IMAGES
of America

BRIARCLIFF LODGE

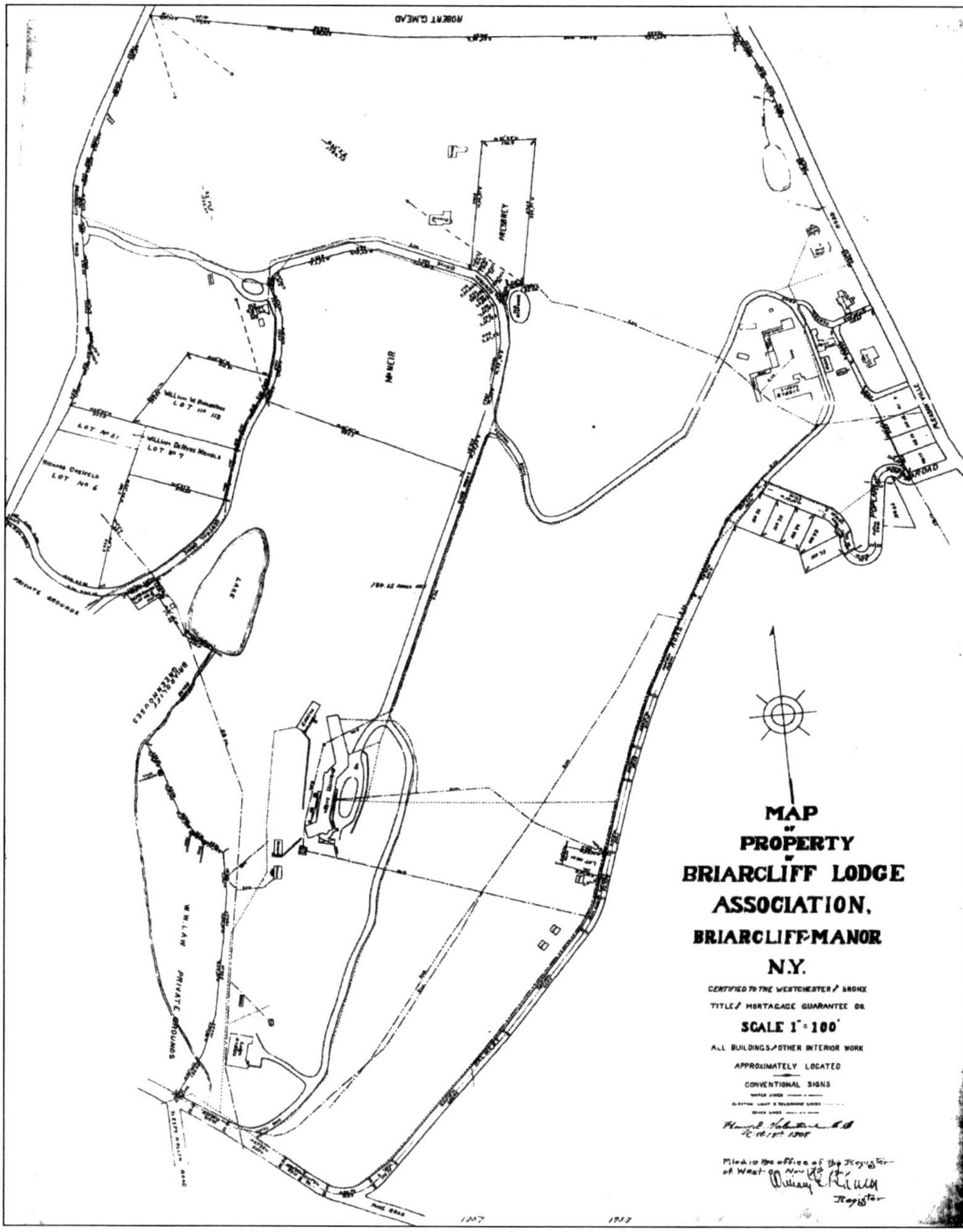

A Henry Valentine Map of Property of Briarcliff Lodge Association, 1907. The Briarcliff Lodge Association was a company formed by owner Walter Law to manage the hotel operations. The core campus was bordered by Scarborough Road on the south (at bottom), Dalmeny Road on the east, Central Drive on the north, and Briarcliff Road on the west. The lodge is visible at the bottom, left of center. The casino, helps' cottages, and lodge stables are west of the lodge. The Briarcliff Farms office, print shop, Table Water Company, stable complex, and former Stillman residence are at the upper right, on Pleasantville Road. The lodge golf course started at the parapet outside the lodge and went east to Dalmeny Road, north, and then west behind Central Drive to Briarcliff Road and back to the lodge near the lake.

IMAGES
of America

BRIARCLIFF LODGE

Rob Yasinsac

ARCADIA
PUBLISHING

ISBN 978-0-7385-3620-0

Published by Arcadia Publishing
Charleston, South Carolina

Printed in the United States of America

Library of Congress Catalog Card Number: 2004104493

For all general information contact Arcadia Publishing at:
Telephone 843-853-2070
Fax 843-853-0044
E-mail sales@arcadiapublishing.com
For customer service and orders:
Toll-Free 1-888-313-2665

Visit us on the Internet at www.arcadiapublishing.com

A BRIARCLIFF LODGE ADVERTISEMENT. The bovine pictured here represented the 1,200 head of Jersey bulls and cows of Briarcliff Farms in 1902. Dairy products from Briarcliff Farms won international acclaim in the years preceding the construction of Briarcliff Lodge. The distinction of quality and product superiority also described the hotel, which opened in 1902. Arthur Bave managed the lodge in its first year. David B. Plumer succeeded him and managed the lodge during its expansion period, between 1907 and 1909.

CONTENTS

ACKNOWLEDGMENTS

This book would not have been possible without the support and assistance of those who cherished Briarcliff Lodge and wished to see it preserved. I thank the scores of people who have taken the time to contact me regarding Briarcliff Lodge.

The following individuals and organizations provided photographs and research assistance for this book or gave me a ride to the lodge to help take more photographs. I am greatly indebted to Andrew Allen; Jack Bakker; Carol Haddad and the Briarcliff Manor-Scarborough Historical Society; Rachel Davis; Ian Gall; Mark Jelley; Karl Xydexx Jorgensen; Susan Czarnecki and the King's College; Ed and Ginger Kuhlman; Dyan Wapnick, Rod Davis and the Little Nine Partners Historical Society; Gigi Carnes, Merestead; Rob Miller; the New-York Historical Society; Roberta Arminio, Debra Van Steen and the Ossining Historical Society; Michael Seneca and the Philadelphia Architects and Buildings Project, the Athenaeum of Philadelphia; Tim Rice; Tom Rinaldi; Richard Smiraldi; Peter Cutul, Elizabeth Fuller, Katie Hite, Chris Marinaro, and the Westchester County Historical Society; Stefanie Valenzky; Eileen O'Connor-Weber; Robert Worth; and Dave Whitehead and Rachel Carr.

Thanks to Jim Logan for legal advice and to Thom Johnson for use of his darkroom. Standard Printing of Bridgeport, Connecticut, provided scanning services. Bill Burton read an early draft of the book and provided many helpful suggestions for the text; he also shared images from his postcard collection.

Two of the Briarcliff Manor-Scarborough Historical Society's books, *A Village Between Two Rivers*, presented by the Briarcliff Manor-Scarborough Historical Society, and *The Changing Landscape: A History of Briarcliff Manor-Scarborough*, by Mary Cheever, were highly informative resources for this project.

Sandi Schneider provided hotel-era photographs and news clippings from the family scrapbook. Her dad, Frederick Steele, a valuable source of information, grew up in Briarcliff Lodge when his father, Chauncey Depew Steele, was the manager.

Michael Molinelli, architect, compiled a detailed survey showing that Briarcliff Lodge could be saved. I am grateful to reproduce in part his essay about the fire. The article, appearing in this book at the beginning of chapter 7, was originally published in entirety in three issues of *Here at Home* (November 2003 to January 2004).

Photographs in chapters 6, 7, and 8 are by the author unless otherwise noted. Photographs courtesy of Sandi Schneider were usually taken by Underwood and Underwood, or Helm, and used in many of the Briarcliff Lodge publicity brochures.

Last but not least, I am indebted to my editor, Pam O'Neil, who believed in this project and brought it through.

INTRODUCTION

For 101 years, a most magnificent building stood in the heart of Westchester County. Embracing the finest elements of domestic architecture of its time, Briarcliff Lodge was a resort hotel that catered to future U.S. presidents, New York State governors, foreign dignitaries, business leaders, movie stars, and professional athletes. The lodge was also the scene of many memorable occasions for local residents, who attended weddings, receptions, and dances in the ballroom, Dutch Kitchen, and Stone Dining Room.

Surrounding the hotel were dairy farms and greenhouses. The milk, water, and roses were sold to first-class hotels and restaurants in New York City and even served on transatlantic voyages. Briarcliff Lodge and the surrounding farms gave birth to the village of Briarcliff Manor, which incorporated in 1902, the year the lodge opened.

In later years, Briarcliff Lodge served as a center of higher learning for two private institutions: Edgewood Park School and the King's College. Both schools preserved the historic integrity of the hotel by maintaining architectural details and original furnishings. All the while, many of those who went to school there or lived nearby grew strongly attached to this building.

Briarcliff Lodge was abandoned after the King's College closed its doors in December 1994, and plans for the lodge's adaptive reuse were strongly contested. Yet, the old hotel retained much of its original architectural and structural integrity into the 21st century. Several concerned citizens acted to save Briarcliff Lodge in its centennial. Finally, in 2003, village officials approved a development plan for the property, which included the demolition of Briarcliff Lodge. On September 20, 2003, the original 1902 wood-frame structure burned to the ground.

My interest in Briarcliff Lodge is part of a larger effort to document decaying historic sites in New York State's Hudson River Valley. Here we have lost too many significant places. Resorts, brickyards, factories, churches, schools, and homes are important, as they create a sense of place and help define our history and identity. These historic sites continue to disappear at an alarming pace as the region undergoes another wave of physical change in the early 21st century, but it has been shown over and over again that it is never too late to save a neglected building. The preservation of historic buildings offers tangible and intangible benefits to a community that new construction often cannot. I hope that my photographs will inspire preservation, reuse, and protection of these important places.

—Rob Yasinsac
Tarrytown, New York
www.hudsonvalleyruins.org
April 2004

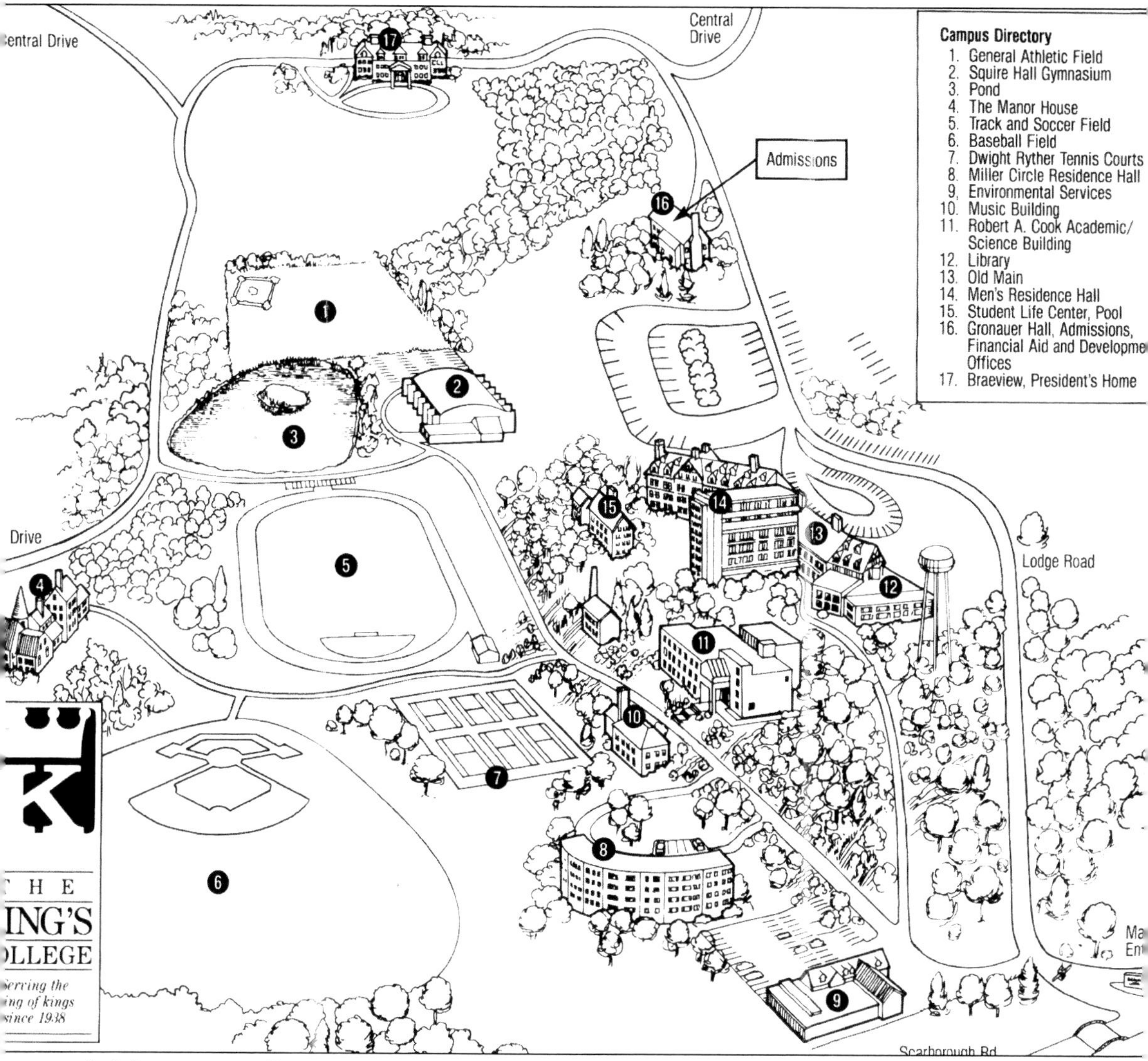

A Map of the Briarcliff Campus, the King's College. The approximately 84-acre campus of the King's College is shown here, with Briarcliff Lodge represented by Nos. 12–14. Many copies of this 1990s-era pamphlet were found inside the abandoned Briarcliff Lodge.

One

Walter Law, "the Laird of Briarcliff Manor" 1890–1901

In the 1890s, a businessman "retired" to central Westchester County, New York, still then very rural, to start a model farm. Over several years he purchased dozens of parcels of land and accumulated 5,200 acres. As part of his plan he erected guest lodgings. The most famous of these lodges opened in 1902, and that hotel grew even larger over the next decade. Also in 1902, a new village was carved out of the middle of it all.

The farm, lodge, and village all shared the name Briarcliff. Walter William Law, the retired businessman, established these enterprises after a career in Westchester's thriving carpet industry. Born in Kidderminster, England, on November 13, 1837, Law immigrated to the United States in January 1860. The son of a carpet dealer, he began working for the W&J Sloane Company one year later. In 1864, Law was the first person to become a traveling salesman for the firm. Two years later he became a partner in the company. Law lived with his wife, Georgianna Ransom Law, and their children in Yonkers, near the large carpet factories for which W&J Sloane acted as selling agents.

In 1890, Walter Law made the Stillman property, Briarcliff Farm, his first purchase in the area. Given the nickname the Laird of Briarcliff Manor by his friend Andrew Carnegie, Law found a "small, worn-out and unprofitable farm" and made it an internationally known operation using existing buildings and constructing new ones. Many of the new structures were designed in the half-timber and stucco Tudor style, a popular theme at that time but perhaps also reminiscent of Law's English roots.

The area in which Law purchased his land was unincorporated and was known as Whitson's Corners, after the Whitson family. John Whitson donated land for the District No. 6 schoolhouse in 1865. The Richard Whitson house was located on Pleasantville Road (it still stands today), and the post office was housed in the Joseph Whitson house. A railroad stop also took the name Whitson's Station. The name Whitson's was replaced by Briarcliff as Law's farm operations expanded in the 1890s.

The name Briarcliff originated from the estate of Rev. John David Ogilby, professor of ecclesiastical history at the General Theological Seminary in New York City. His estate, Brier Cliff, named in honor of his family's home in Ireland, was located near the site of where Briarcliff Lodge was later built. Ogilby commissioned the construction of the All Saints' Episcopal Church on Scarborough Road. Richard Upjohn, architect of Trinity Church in New York City, designed the building and modeled it after the medieval church of Bemerton, in Wiltshire, England.

Although Walter Law's reasons for moving to Briarcliff were mainly for personal health and his family, he began to focus his energy on Briarcliff Farm in 1896 and 1897. His retirement from the carpet business in 1899 made Briarcliff a second career. The design of the farm was a serious, methodical system for manufacturing the best possible farm products for human consumption. In 1900, Law established the School of Practical Agriculture on 66 acres on Pleasantville Road. When the school building opened the following year, students were taught scientific basics of farming and gardening, as well as product conservation and the development of specialty markets for fine goods.

Briarcliff dairy products were advertised as "the highest quality, produced and handled at every point under rigid equipment and approved by the highest scientific authority." Top New York City hotels and restaurants served Briarcliff milk to guests. The Briarcliff Farms store had several successive locations in New York City, including one at the Windsor Arcade. Milk sent on overseas voyages was still consumed fresh on return trips.

In 1907, Law said of Briarcliff, "I did not find an ideal condition in the country. Yet, it has been given to me to work it out and make an ideal country life up here, which I have been endeavoring to do. . . . I have strong conviction that with the golden rule always in the ascendant Briarcliff Manor will go on to increase in numbers and moral power, each member of it as one happy family, filled with charity and thoughtful consideration for his neighbor, and above all, having the blessing of the lord. 'It maketh rich and addeth no sorrow.' A veritable Garden of Eden, where God himself will love to dwell."

ALL SAINTS' EPISCOPAL CHURCH. Construction of this church began in 1848. The first services were held on December 13, 1854, three years after Rev. John David Ogilby died. All Saints' Episcopal Church was the only structure built on the original Brier Cliff estate to be listed on the National Register of Historic Places, a recognition that was never requested for the great Briarcliff Lodge. (Courtesy of the Ossining Historical Society.)

WHITSON'S SCHOOLHOUSE, DISTRICT NO. 6. This one-room schoolhouse was built in 1865 on land donated by John Whitson. George A. Todd Jr. served as superintendent and teacher from at least 1867 through 1906. A post office was established in 1881, and the intersection of Unionville (later Pleasantville) and South State Roads was named Whitson's Corners. (Courtesy of the Ossining Historical Society.)

Briarcliff Farm, Property of James Stillman, Sing Sing, 1886. Walter Law purchased this 232-acre farm, located between Pleasantville and Briarcliff Roads, in 1890 for $35,000. (Courtesy of the Westchester County Historical Society.)

The Stillman Residence. The right side of the house has been torn down and is now the site of the Church of St. Theresa, built between 1927 and 1928. (Courtesy of the Briarcliff Manor-Scarborough Historical Society.)

WALTER LAW. A controlling force in the life of Walter Law was a motto given to him by his father when he was eight or nine years old: "If a Cobbler by trade, I'll make it my pride to be the best of all Cobblers to be; and if only a Tinker, no Tinker on earth shall mend an old kettle like me." Law invested some $2.5 million in Briarcliff by 1902, when Briarcliff Lodge was built. (Courtesy of the Ossining Historical Society.)

WALTER LAW AND OTHERS. Walter and Georgianna Ransom had six children, including three daughters—Martha, Carolyn, and Edith. Two of the sons were Walter Law Jr., who served as chairman of the state tax commission under Gov. Nathan L. Miller, and Henry Law, who managed the Briarcliff Lodge Association. The sixth child died at a very young age. The man standing is believed to be Walter Law Jr. (Courtesy of the Ossining Historical Society.)

THE WALTER LAW MANSION. The Manor House was Walter Law's home. It was built a short walk away from where Briarcliff Lodge was later constructed. Across Scarborough Road, Law built homes for three of his children: Edith Law Brockelman (Mount Vernon), Walter W. Law Jr. (Six Gables), and Henry Law. (Courtesy of the Ossining Historical Society.)

THE WALTER LAW STONE WALL. The stone wall on Scarborough Road in front of Walter Law's home is shown here. Large stone lions atop the gate pillars were added much later, and the wall still stands.

BRIARCLIFF CONGREGATIONAL CHURCH, SOUTH STATE ROAD. The Congregational church was built in 1896 following a request from George Todd to Walter Law for a larger and permanent home. The congregational nature of the church incorporated the various beliefs among those living on Walter Law's farm. Law continued to support the church in later years. The edifice was enlarged in 1905. Law donated Japanese lanterns and four Tiffany stained-glass memorial windows. (Courtesy of the Ossining Historical Society.)

THE DYSART HOUSE. The first guest lodging built by Walter Law opened in 1896 on Pleasantville Road opposite the railroad station. The architectural style of the Dysart House foreshadowed Briarcliff Lodge; it had a stone foundation, an upper story of half-timber and stucco, dormer windows built into the roof, and gables with pointed wood finials. The building was converted to Misses Tewksbury's School after Briarcliff Lodge opened in 1902 and later Miss Marshall's School. (Courtesy of the Briarcliff Manor-Scarborough Historical Society.)

BRIARCLIFF FARMS OFFICE, PLEASANTVILLE ROAD. The main dairy complex was at the north end of Dalmeny Road, adjacent to the farm office shown here. Barn A, a livery stable and blacksmith, and wheelwright and harness shops stood here, as did the Briarcliff Print Shop and the Briarcliff Table Water Company. (Courtesy of the Briarcliff Manor-Scarborough Historical Society.)

BRIARCLIFF FARMS OFFICE RUINS. The Tudor-style building on Pleasantville Road burned in 1901 and was rebuilt in 1902 in the Shingle style. Walter Law's personal office was in this building. It later housed the offices of the Briarcliff Realty Company. The building was once again redesigned and rebuilt in the mid-1960s, when it became the offices of the International Union of Operating Engineers. (Courtesy of the Ossining Historical Society.)

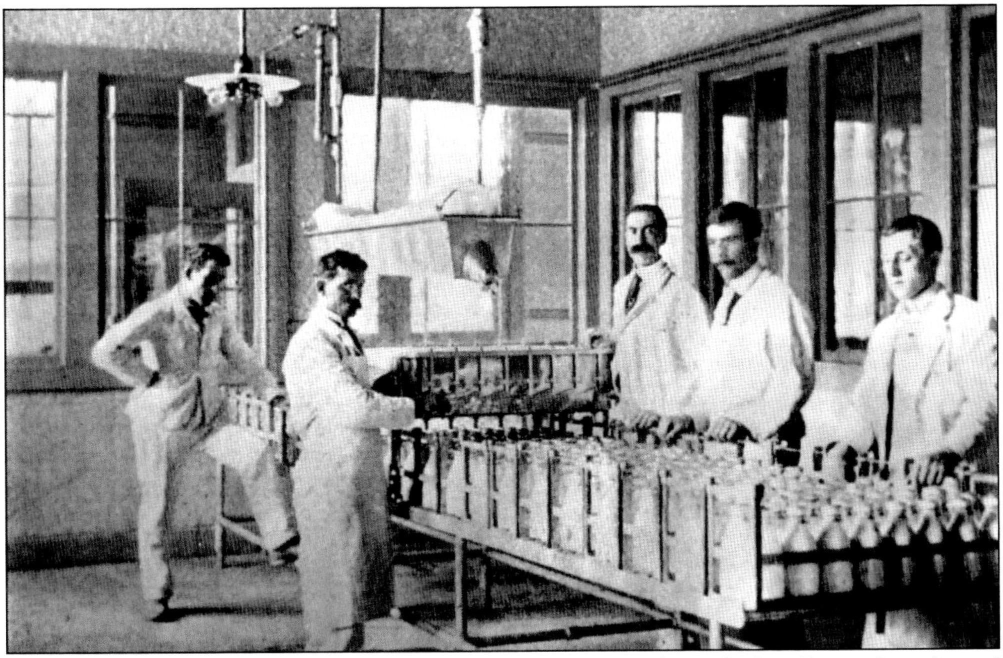

MILK PROCESSING. Walter Law encouraged cleanliness and gentle handling of cattle and gave awards to workers who best demonstrated those characteristics. These practices "resulted in a more thorough understanding of the true value of pure milk and the safeguards which must surround its production and handling." Farm employees were frequently lectured on the topics of cleanliness and the "evils of contaminated milk." (Courtesy of the Briarcliff Manor-Scarborough Historical Society.)

A DAIRY BARN INTERIOR. Cleanliness was important to stop the transfer of diseases from animals to humans. In 1902, Dr. Garnault of Paris inoculated himself with bovine tuberculosis and subsequently developed tumors, disproving a theory that humans were not susceptible to bovine disease. The *Briarcliff Outlook*, a promotional newspaper, wrote that "care and treatment of cows should be such that disease cannot develop," protecting cattle and ultimately the consumers of the farm products. (Courtesy of the Briarcliff Manor-Scarborough Historical Society.)

THE PLASMON COMPANY OF AMERICA, WOODSIDE AVENUE. Here, skimmed milk was converted into plasmon, a powdery food preparation, "the most nutritious food known to modern science." Author Mark Twain was acting president of the company in 1907, when it went bankrupt. The Briarcliff Laundry, the Briarcliff Manor Light and Power Company, and a Briarcliff Farms Dairy were also located on Woodside Avenue. (Courtesy of the Briarcliff Manor-Scarborough Historical Society.)

THE SCHOOL OF PRACTICAL AGRICULTURE, POCANTICO LODGE. Construction of the school building was completed in the spring of 1901. The school moved to upstate New York in 1903, and for two years the building was a small year-round hotel known as Pocantico Lodge, under the management of Briarcliff Lodge. It became Mrs. Knox's School in 1905. The Pocantico Lodge burned in 1912.

Two

THE HOTEL BEAUTIFUL 1902–1922

For the design of Briarcliff Lodge, Walter Law hired Philadelphia-based architect Guy King. Law instructed King to design a hotel that looked not so much like a hotel but was "aesthetically pure in type," containing the "atmosphere of a cultivated gentleman's home." A graduate of the Atelier Girard in Paris, King returned to Philadelphia, and in 1885 established an office with Moses Arnold. By 1896, he was working independently and specialized in resort cottage and bungalow architecture. By the time he died in 1925, he had designed over 100 known projects, including residences, banks, stores, and factories in Pennsylvania, New Jersey, New York, and elsewhere. He also designed hospitals through his involvement with the International Red Cross.

King designed a number of buildings in Westchester County, including farm residences, a stable, and hitching sheds for the Briarcliff Farms. He also designed a pumping station for the American Pipe Company along the nearby Pocantico River. The builders of the lodge were S. Wood Cornell and the Briarcliff Construction Company of Pleasantville.

The brick, stucco, and half-timber Tudor style of the lodge became popular in the United States in the 1890s. The main facade of the lodge was two stories tall, while third- and fourth-floor dormer windows peppered the roofline, occasionally interrupted by cross-pitch gables. "In [Briarcliff Lodge] was to be placed every convenience, and every device which modern luxury demands. Without it was to be a dream of architectural beauty; within, an illustration of the refined and artistic era in which we live."

The Briarcliff grounds, designed by the Olmsted firm, were "acknowledged to be one of the most highly improved park forms in America." Founded by Frederick Law Olmsted (no relation to Walter Law), one of America's preeminent 19th-century landscape architects and co-designer of Central Park in New York City, the firm designed many projects in the surrounding area, including private estates for Frank Vanderlip (Beechwood), Margaret Louisa Vanderbilt Shepard (Woodlea), James Speyer, and E. W. Harden.

Coinciding with the opening of the lodge in 1902 was the formation of the village of Briarcliff Manor. Walter Law tried unsuccessfully to incorporate Scarborough in 1899. Shortly after, houses were constructed near Briarcliff Lodge for farm workers, and Law had enough residents to incorporate. On November 21, 1902, 25 taxpayers voted unanimously in favor of incorporating as the village of Briarcliff Manor. William De Nyse Nichols was elected as the first village president on December 19.

In 1902, Walter Law owned all the land in the mile-square village, except two small parcels. He also employed nearly all of the 100 or so residents of the village. In addition to the farms, guest lodgings, and employee housing, Law provided for a new church and a new railroad station. Ultimately, his interest in Briarcliff was real estate. The hotel, churches, schools, railroad station, and new house served as vehicles to promote the sale of numerous tracts of land for residential development. The model farm gave way to a model "English Countryside community" when Briarcliff Farms left Westchester County for Dutchess County in 1907.

As Briarcliff Manor grew, so did the hotel. A north wing was completed in 1907, and a seven-story west wing was added in 1909. The new extensions were built of steel and concrete and designed to be fireproof. The year 1909 saw major improvements of facilities on the lodge grounds as well, and the lodge began to keep its doors open year-round. To more efficiently manage the expanding operations, Walter Law formed the Briarcliff Lodge Association to run the hotel and recreational facilities, incorporated the Briarcliff Farms, and formed the Briarcliff Realty Company to oversee the sale of newly vacated farmland.

The year 1909 was also marked by the Hudson-Fulton Celebration, which commemorated the tercentennial of Henry Hudson's first voyage on the river that now bears his name, and the centennial of the launch of the first steamship, the *Clermont*, which plied the Hudson River as well. Briarcliff Lodge was in top condition for the thousands of tourists who passed through its doors. By the end of the first decade of the century, Briarcliff Lodge had firmly established itself as the premiere resort in the Hudson Valley, if not the country.

Briarcliff Lodge

BRIARCLIFF MANOR, N. Y.

The "Hotel Beautiful" of the Westchester Hill Country

Now Open for the Summer

DAVID B. PLUMER, *Manager*

¶ Briarcliff Manor, less than thirty miles from New York City, is a choicely improved spot of country with natural charm unspoiled by noise or smoke of factory. The Lodge is complete and perfect in its entertaining facilities and from its heights commands a broad view of the lordly Hudson, the Palisades and the blue distant Catskills. Beauty of scenery, stone roads for coaching or auto touring, a fine golf course, with a full list of open air attractions have given the place pre-eminent advantages among resorts easily reached from New York.

¶ For Briarcliff Lodge—Wall Street patrons use Ninth Avenue Elevated, connecting at 155th Street with Putnam Division, New York Central, to Briarcliff Manor; or from Grand Central Station, Hudson River line to Scarborough.

A BRIARCLIFF LODGE ADVERTISEMENT, PRE-1907. "Situated on one of the most beautiful eminences of picturesque Westchester County, six hundred feet above tide water, and twenty-nine miles from New York City, stands the Briar Cliff Lodge. From its broad verandas, its vine covered pergola, and its many windows, there is afforded a panorama of the majestic Hudson for a dozen miles, with three distinct ranges of the lower Catskills shutting in the western horizon beyond. To the east, the north and south are the wooded Westchester hills, the rivals of the Berkshires. Immediately in the foreground and stretching to the Hudson a mile away are the great estates of Walter W. Law, James Speyer, V. Everit Macy, William Rockefeller and others, which from the commanding height of the lodge are to be seen in all their natural beauty and perfection. In every direction, as far as the eye can reach, the country is unblemished with factory, town or anything which would mar the natural attractiveness of the most exclusive region of New York State." (Quoted material from the *Ossining Democratic Register*, May 27, 1903.)

BRIARCLIFF LODGE, PRE-1907. The newly completed hotel opened its doors to paying guests for the first time on June 26, 1902, under the management of Arthur Bave. The original hotel was a wood-frame structure containing approximately 75 guest rooms. The lodge grounds were decorated by Japanese lanterns, obtained by Walter Law from missionaries. The water tower in the rear was constructed by the Chicago Bridge and Iron Company. (Courtesy of Bill Burton.)

BARN C, DALMENY ROAD. Barns B and C were located here at the south end of Dalmeny Road, just below Briarcliff Lodge. Barn D stood at Beech Hill Road and Route 117. Barn E was on Pleasantville Road and east of the Taconic Parkway, and Barn F stood on Saw Mill River Road. Houses for farm workers were also built along Dalmeny Road. Briarcliff Lodge is visible at the top. (Courtesy of the Briarcliff Manor-Scarborough Historical Society.)

ARISTOCRAT, A JERSEY BULL, BARN C. By 1904, there were 2,460 head of Jersey cattle, uncounted numbers of poultry and pigs, and 300 workers on the farm. Purebred Jersey cows produced several thousand quarts of milk daily. Briarcliff cream and milk won a gold medal at the Paris Exposition in 1900. Farmlands were also reserved for grains such as corn, rye, and oats; apple orchards; and vegetable gardens. (Courtesy of the Briarcliff Manor-Scarborough Historical Society.)

BRIARCLIFF LODGE, PRE-1909. "[Briarcliff Lodge is] a modern manor house in the beautiful country of the lower Hudson, less than an hour from New York, with riding, golf links, tennis courts and every opportunity for rest and recreation." (Hotel brochure.) Although the exterior Tudor design of Briarcliff Lodge was ornamental, the original section was built with heavy timber framing. (Courtesy of the Westchester County Historical Society.)

AN AERIAL VIEW OF THE NORTH WING. The 1907 addition to the north side of the original lodge was constructed in a fashion sympathetic to the original structure. Capacity then reached approximately 150 rooms; the interior layout of the first floor was altered in the early 1900s, and the number of rooms varied. This view was most likely taken from the tower extension. John Udall Clark built the extensions in 1907 and 1909.

BRIARCLIFF LODGE, FROM THE EAST, PRE-1909. "Surely the builders of the Lodge have no error in its location, standing as it does upon the highest ridge for miles around, and commanding the widest sweep of the valley and river from its wide verandas." (*Briarcliff Outlook.*) This view shows the lodge after the 1907 north wing was built but before the tower was added. (Courtesy of Laura Lee Keating.)

"BEAUTIFUL BRIARCLIFF LODGE," POST-1909. Guy King designed a 72-room, seven-story addition on the steeply sloping hillside to the west. The roof was intended to be used as an aerial wharf for airships. Thus, Briarcliff Lodge gained the distinction of having the world's first aerial pier built for the embarkation of voyages by dirigibles. It is not known to have been used for this purpose. (Courtesy of the Briarcliff Manor-Scarborough Historical Society.)

BRIARCLIFF LODGE WITH GREENHOUSES. Private greenhouses behind Walter Law's home, managed by William McGowan, produced decorations for the entire Briarcliff Farms, including Briarcliff Lodge, Law's own mansion, and the small-frame employee cottages. Law awarded prizes to the workers with the best-kept cottage gardens. On average, 20 men worked at the greenhouses and flowerbeds, while 100 men were employed when new gardens were laid out around the lodge. (Courtesy of Laura Lee Keating.)

THE PIERSON GREENHOUSES. The commercial greenhouses operated by Paul M. Pierson, located between Sleepy Hollow and what is now Fountain Road, were devoted to the American Beauty rose and other rare carnations for the market. Foreman George Romaine first propagated the famous pink Briarcliff rose here. Roses shipped to Scotland were received fresh 18 days later. Between 5,000 and 8,000 roses per week were cut at the greenhouses. (Courtesy of the Ossining Historical Society.)

"A FIRE ENGINE AT BRIARCLIFF LODGE, FREDERICK MESSINGER." In 1901, Frederick Messinger organized the Briarcliff Steamer Company No. 1. The Briarcliff Realty Company purchased a steam-operated pumper and a hose wagon, which were stored at the Barn A complex of Briarcliff Farms. Some of the biggest fires the early company fought were the Knox School fire in 1912 and the "Great Barn Fire" of April 28, 1913. (Courtesy of the Ossining Historical Society.)

THE GREAT BARN FIRE, APRIL 28, 1913. The dairy barn at the north end of Dalmeny Road, next door to the fire department, was one of the early fires in the village's history. (Courtesy of the Briarcliff Manor-Scarborough Historical Society.)

THE FIREMEN'S PARADE, 1908. The fire department's first parade passed the great Briarcliff Lodge. The hotel was not strictly an enclave for the exclusive, but it hosted many community events in its century of existence. (Courtesy of the Briarcliff Manor-Scarborough Historical Society.)

A HORSE TANDEM. The Briarcliff Lodge offered a variety of conveyances to guests over the years, providing service between the railroad stations at Scarborough and Briarcliff to the lodge. The Briarcliff roadways were made of perfectly conditioned macadam, lined with cement drains, and surrounded by stone fences. (Courtesy of the Ossining Historical Society.)

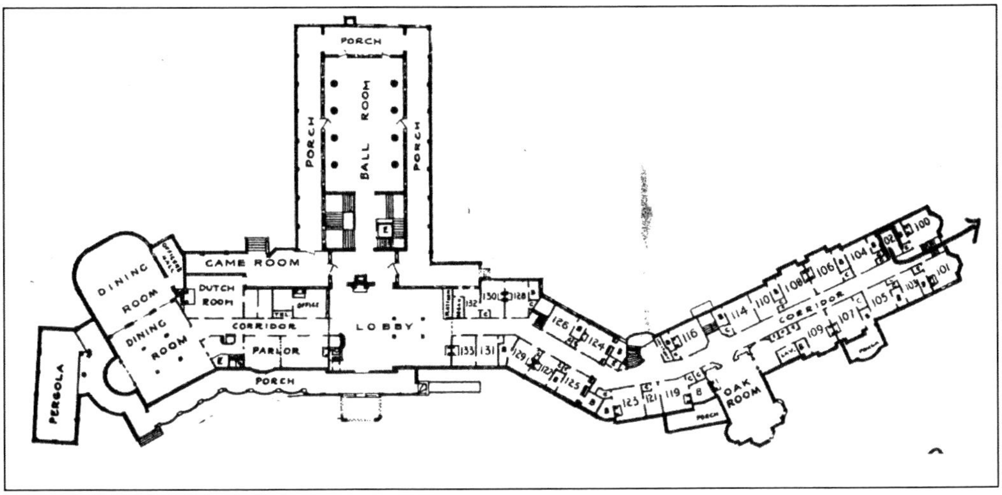

THE FIRST-FLOOR PLAN AND THE FOURTH-FLOOR PLAN. These plans show the layout of Briarcliff Lodge at its full extant in the hotel era. By 1909, the lodge had 221 guest rooms. The hotel was lighted by electricity and offered elevator service. A system of suction wheels in the attic of the lodge provided active ventilation for closets and bathrooms, something not installed in any other hotel in the country at that time.

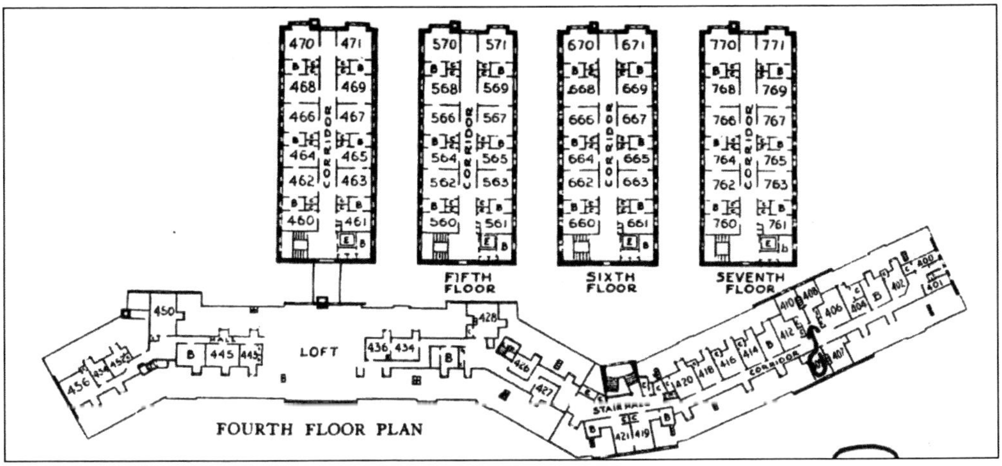

THE GREAT HALL. The interior of the lodge was designed in full accord with the beauty of its exterior. The Great Hall, or lobby, featured a large fieldstone fireplace, a tiled fireplace, and an Aeolian organ. Armor and medieval weapons decorated the Great Hall in the early hotel period. (Courtesy of the Ossining Historical Society.)

THE DUTCH ROOM. "Holland has contributed much of the furnishings of the Dutch kitchen, which is rich in Rembrandt effects and a veritable treasure room of rare China paintings and articles of verdu." (*Briarcliff Outlook.*) Rough adze-hewn timbers, a hipped ceiling, and an "enormous cozy fireplace" were decorated with etchings from England and oil paintings by European and American artists. The design of the room was based on a restaurant in Edam, the Netherlands.

The Ballroom. Classical fluted columns (topped with Ionic capitals) and Italian marble walls provided a refined setting for parties and dances. Madame Lillian Nordica sang here on September 22, 1911, to an audience including John D. and Laura Spelman Rockefeller, Frank A. and Narcissa Cox Vanderlip, John D. and Annie Mills Archbold, and Chauncey M. and May Palmer Depew, among many other prominent businessmen who lived in the area. Thomas A. Edison was honored here in 1909. (Courtesy of the Ossining Historical Society.)

The Veranda. The ballroom, located on the first floor of the tower extension, opened on three sides to this veranda. (Photograph by William Hale Kirk Company, courtesy of the Ossining Historical Society.)

The Library. "The Lodge library, a home-like apartment in warm colors, is well supplied with popular books and richly and suitably furnished." (*Briarcliff Outlook.*) The room was adjacent on the north of the large dining room and contained one of the tiled fireplace mantels. (Courtesy of the Briarcliff Manor-Scarborough Historical Society.)

The Steam Plant. A steam plant built in 1909 below the lodge heated the hotel and sterilized water for drinking and cooking, using equipment from the Standard Steam Specialty Company. The new steam plant was built so that the tremendous traffic of coal and ashes would no longer go to the hotel; the transfer of materials was an objectionable practice to guests. (Courtesy of the Briarcliff Manor-Scarborough Historical Society.)

THE AMUSEMENT BUILDING. At the north end of the lodge a smaller Shingle-style building was constructed as an amusement building. It was referred to as the Casino in the early 1900s, when gambling took place here. In the 1920s and 1930s, it was renamed the Health Annex. It contained a bowling alley, squash court, shuffleboard, an indoor swimming pool and locker rooms, and a darkroom for guests who enjoyed amateur photography. (Courtesy of Bill Burton.)

THE INDOOR SWIMMING POOL. The porcelain-lined pool in the amusement building was supplied with water from the artesian wells in the field opposite the steam plant. The pool measured 30 by 70 feet and varied in depth from 4 to 10 feet. (Courtesy of Sandi Schneider.)

Briarcliff Garage. Originally the lodge stables, this building became the garage when mass-produced automobiles, including Lozier limousines and Maxwell "big fours," became popular means for surveying the hills and valleys of Westchester County. The garage was enlarged and rebuilt from the inside in 1909. The early 20th century was a time of incredible scientific advances, yet many guests still preferred horse-drawn carriages. At the same time, the lodge was planning for the day when airships would deliver visitors to its roof.

Joe Seymour Racing Car No. 21, Simplex, April 24, 1908. Walter Law sponsored this 256-mile Briarcliff Trophy Race through Briarcliff, Millwood, Mount Kisco, Armonk, Valhalla, and Eastview. Twenty-two cars representing 16 manufacturers from five countries competed. Lewis Strang finished the eight-lap course first, driving an Isotta in 5 hours, 14 minutes, and 13 seconds. He averaged 46 miles per hour on the unpaved roads. Over 300,000 spectators watched the race. (Courtesy of the Westchester County Historical Society.)

MRS. DOW'S SCHOOL. In 1903, Mary Elizabeth Dow started a school for girls at the Briarcliff Lodge. In 1905, Walter Law gave the school 35 acres and a new home on Elm Road. The architect of the brick building was H. (Harold) Van Buren Magonigle, who also designed the Firemen's Memorial in Riverside Park, New York City. (Courtesy of Bill Burton.)

BRIARCLIFF MANOR RAILROAD STATION. Walter Law built this station for the Putnam Division of the New York Central Railroad in 1906 in the same style as Briarcliff Lodge. Flowers, oriental rugs, and mission furnishings decorated the interior. An earlier station on this location was moved farther northeast, to Millwood. A trip from Briarcliff Manor to the 15th Street terminus of the Sixth and Ninth Elevated Railroad took 65 minutes. (Courtesy of Bill Burton.)

BRIARCLIFF TABLE WATER COMPANY. Originating in a natural spring 250 feet below the surface, the water was "bottled at the mouth of the well at Briarcliff Farms," served to guests at the lodge, and sold at Briarcliff Farms' stores in New York City. Walter Law steered clear of misleading advertising claims of the day: "There's no sulphur or Perpetual youth, or Medicinal theory about it. Just Purity and Safety in water and handling." (Courtesy of the Ossining Historical Society.)

THE DALMENY HOUSE. The Dalmeny House was a boardinghouse for unmarried men who worked on the farm. It featured a large, airy dining room, a well-stocked waiting room, and amusement was encouraged through suitable games provided to the men. Walter Law frequently visited the workers and arranged for readings and lectures. Built on Dalmeny Road, it was moved "month by month" in 1909 to the Briarcliff Lodge property, near two small "helps' cottages." It was later named Harmony Hall.

WALTER LAW WITH CORNSTALKS IN DUTCHESS COUNTY. Briarcliff Farms moved to Pine Plains, Dutchess County, New York, in 1907, when Walter Law purchased 3,249 acres. The Briarcliff Manor lands offered limited agricultural opportunities, and real estate values encouraged Law to sell the former farm lands for residential development. George W. Tuttle supervised the purchase and development of the new farm. Walter Law sold the farm at Pine Plains in 1918. (Courtesy of the Little Nine Partners Historical Society.)

THE BRIARCLIFF REALTY COMPANY, BRIARCLIFF LODGE ASSOCIATION. The realty company, presided over by Henry H. Law until 1936 and then his son Theodore, sold much of the acreage owned by the Briarcliff Lodge Association after the farm operations moved to Dutchess County. This image dates from the 1930s. These realtors were photographed in front of the offices of the Briarcliff Realty on Pleasantville Road. They were supporting the National Recovery Administration. (Courtesy of the Ossining Historical Society.)

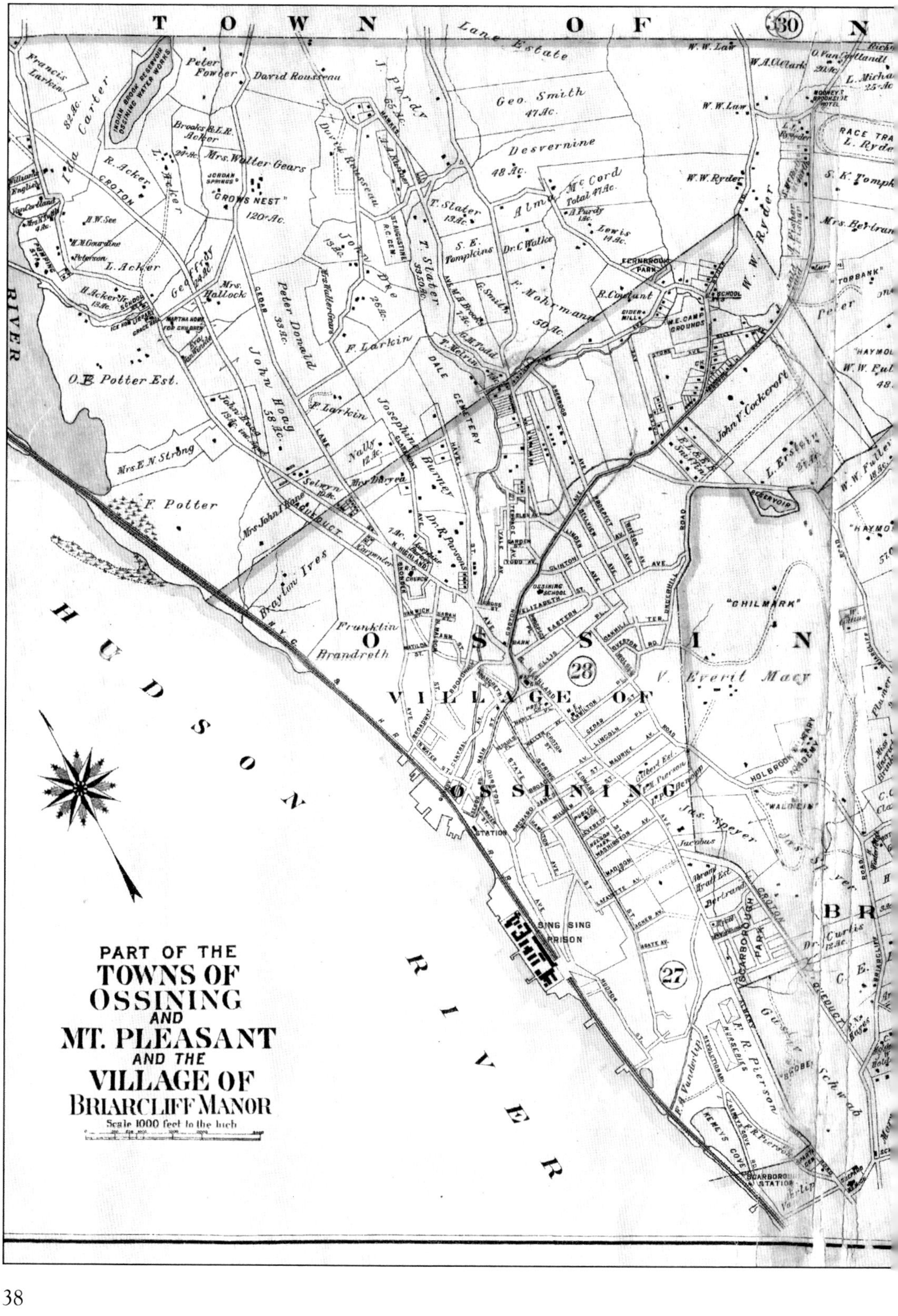
PART OF THE
TOWNS OF
OSSINING
AND
MT. PLEASANT
AND THE
VILLAGE OF
BRIARCLIFF MANOR
Scale 1000 feet to the inch
TOWN OF N
30
VILLAGE OF OSSINING
HUDSON RIVER
RIVER
28
27
Lane Estate
Geo. Smith 47 Ac.
Desvernine 48 Ac.
David Rousseau
Peter Fowler
Francis Larkin
Ida Carter 82 Ac.
INDIAN BROOK RESERVOIR OSSINING WATER WORKS
Mrs. Walter Gears
"CROWS NEST" 120 Ac.
O.F. Potter Est.
F. Potter
Mrs. E. N. Strong
John Hoag 58 Ac.
Peter Donald 33 Ac.
F. Larkin
Josephine Burney
Dr. R. Parsons
Braytan Ives
Franklin Brandreth
T. Slater
S. E. Tompkins
F. Mohrmann 50 Ac.
John V. Cockcroft
L. Erstein
W. W. Ryder
W. W. Law
"CHILMARK"
V. Everit Macy
Jas. Speyer
"WALDHEIM"
HOLBROOK MILITARY ACADEMY
SING SING PRISON
STATION
F. R. Pierson
Gustav Schwab
F. A. Vanderlip
KEMEYS COVE
SCARBOROUGH STATION
SCARBOROUGH PARK
OSSINING SCHOOL
M. E. CAMP GROUNDS
FERNBROOK PARK
DALE CEMETERY
RESERVOIR
RACE TRACK L. Ryder
Dr. Curtis 12 Ac.

A MAP OF THE TOWN OF OSSINING, 1911. The extensive landholdings of Walter W. Law are shown here.

BRIARCLIFF LODGE THIRD SEPTEMBER SUNDAY NINETEEN-NINE

BRIARCLIFF ONCE-A-WEEK

TELLING OF NEW YORK'S MOST ACCESSIBLE AND ATTRACTIVE SUBURBAN RESORT HOTEL IN SUMMER AND WINTER SEASON AND OF THE IDEAL VILLAGE COMMUNITY GROWING ABOUT ITS LOCATION

PUBLISHED AT BRIARCLIFF MANOR, NEW YORK

THE *BRIARCLIFF* ONCE-A-WEEK. The *Briarcliff Once-a-Week* and its earlier incarnation, the *Briarcliff Outlook*, were edited by Arthur Emerson and produced at the Briarcliff Print Shop. They contained agricultural articles, a "who's who" listing of weekly hotel guests, and box scores for the Briarcliff Lodge baseball team.

Three

CHAUNCEY DEPEW STEELE 1923–1933

Walter Law worked hard to establish Briarcliff Lodge as a top resort in the Hudson Valley. As a result, wealthy elites summered there and returned to New York City for the winter. Briarcliff Lodge was a favored New York resort in the second decade of the 20th century and the 1920s, eclipsing for a while the famous mountain houses in the nearby Catskills, but eventually Briarcliff would face the struggle to survive as well. Part of Briarcliff's increase in business was a shift to focus on athletics and year-round hostelry.

In 1923, the Law family turned over management of Briarcliff Lodge to Chauncey Depew Steele, who signed a 20-year lease. Henry Law, president and mayor of the village from 1918 until his death in 1936, continued to oversee the Briarcliff Lodge Association, which owned the lodge and leased it to Steele. In January 1924, Walter Law died in Somerville, North Carolina, at the age of 87.

Born in 1890 in New Rochelle, New York, Chauncey Depew Steele was the son of Frederick Albert Steele and Caroline Marie Steele. Frederick, a prominent real estate man in New Rochelle, was noted for his collection of early editions of American literature, including the works of Edgar Allen Poe. He was also a friend of Theodore Roosevelt, Sir Thomas Lipton, and William Cullen Bryant. Frederick named his last son after New York Central Railroad president Chauncey Depew, former U.S. senator, resident of nearby Peekskill, New York, and also godfather to namesake Chauncey Depew Steele.

Steele studied accounting and at the age of 20 got a job at the Algonquin Hotel in New York City. Within a year he was the assistant manager to Frank Case. After 10 years there, Steele took the opportunity to manage Briarcliff Lodge over the protestations of Case and offers to stay. It was under the management of Chauncey Depew Steele that Briarcliff Lodge achieved its greatest prominence.

Many of the most famous businessmen, politicians, and stars of screen and stage stayed at the lodge. The hotel opened to a wider range of clientele in the 1920s but continued to be a place of respite for the wealthy and famous. Guests of the Briarcliff Lodge from the 1920s and 1930s included New York State governors Franklin Roosevelt and Al Smith, the king and queen of Siam, and Elihu Root. John Campbell (Credit Clearing House president, whose office was the "Campbell Apartment" at New York City's Grand Central Station) and his wife frequently hosted parties at Briarcliff Lodge.

Briarcliff Lodge was promoted as "the St. Moritz of America," with expanded athletic facilities and enhanced sports clubs. New suburbanites for whom membership was an important status joined the various athletic associations, and winter carnivals and sporting exhibitions brought in local residents who sought entertainment and diversion. Briarcliff Lodge hosted top professional athletes on the golf course, tennis courts, and in the swimming pool. A new 6,500-yard, 18-hole professional course opened in 1923, designed by Deveraux Emmett, architect of many leading courses in the United States. Winter ski exhibitions were held on a jump constructed on the first fairway of the golf course. The lodge also had its own outdoor ice hockey team and hosted top collegiate clubs.

Henry Law cited Prohibition as a cause for the decline of hotel business at Briarcliff starting in 1930. The proliferation of automobiles was also a detriment, as visitors no longer came to stay for the entire summer. Chauncey Depew Steele surrendered his lease in February 1933. He later went on to manage the Copley Plaza Hotel in Boston from 1939 to 1944. A "health diet sanitarium" operated at the lodge, and the hotel stayed open through 1936, when it was leased to the Edgewood Park School, a women's junior college and preparatory school. The hotel then opened in the summer months through 1939, and the school operated during the off-season. In 1937, the Briarcliff Lodge Association finally sold the property to Edgewood Park.

CHAUNCEY DEPEW STEELE. Chauncey Depew Steele served as hotel manager from 1923 to 1933, during which time he leased the lodge from the Law family. The hotel grew in fame and service during his era of management. (Courtesy of Sandi Schneider.)

DANCING CLASS. Frederick Steele, shown in the top row second from the left, and Chauncey Depew Steele Jr., in the middle row second from the left, were the sons of the hotel manager. Frederick recalled in later years how he missed his first chance to meet Babe Ruth. It was a rainy day, and his mother took him to the movies instead, thinking Ruth would not come to play golf. Ruth came, to Frederick's dismay. Frederick eventually met Ruth and other celebrities. (Courtesy of Sandi Schneider.)

AN AERIAL VIEW. Under Chauncey Depew Steele's management, the lodge operated year-round. Winter sports were implemented to draw visitors in a business that normally depended on the summer customers. Sleighing, ice-skating, skiing, tobogganing, bob-sledding and snow-shoeing were offered as attractions. The lodge advertisements promoted the winter facilities that could be enjoyed minus the cold weather of the Adirondacks. The Hudson River and Croton Point are visible at the top.

BRIARCLIFF LODGE AND THE FIRST FAIRWAY OF THE GOLF COURSE. The lodge and the first fairway of the golf course are shown "perched on the crest of a hill, with only the wooded ridges beyond and the skies above." (Hotel brochure.) (Courtesy of the Briarcliff Manor-Scarborough Historical Society.)

BRIARCLIFF LODGE, NORTH WING, WEST FRONT. Each individual stone making up the first-floor wall was carefully selected in the nearby woods, with care taken not to "injure the weather properties of the stone, consisting of moss, lichens, etc, all of which remain." Indiana limestone was used for the trimmings. Half-timber with pebble dash decorated the second floor. The red roof shingles and red brick chimneys harmonized with the stonework. (Courtesy of Bill Burton.)

THE PORTE COCHERE. The main entrance to the lodge was the porte cochere on the east front. "Here is seclusion and rest and the stimulating companionship with nature at her best, along with the luxury of the most refined home and the freedom of the forest and hills at your doorstep." (Hotel brochure.) (Courtesy of Sandi Schneider.)

THE EAST FACADE FROM ABOVE. "Where clustering eaves and tall chimneys, each creating its own delightful irregularity, inevitably call to mind the rambling inn of bygone coach days." (Hotel brochure.) (Courtesy of Sandi Schneider.)

THE NORTH END OF THE LODGE. The Health Annex was located at the north end of the lodge. It is visible at the end of the walkway. (Courtesy of Sandi Schneider.)

THE OUTDOOR PERGOLA. The pergola, likened to an Italian pavilion, hosted open-air dancing in season and concerts, which were regularly scheduled events at the hotel. The lodge was also popular as a setting for early silent movies. In 1915, the Daniel Frohman film *The Seven Sisters*, starring Marguerite Clark, was shot at Briarcliff Lodge, which was set as a castle. Tallulah Bankhead, Sarah Bernhardt, and other famous actresses and actors stayed at the lodge. (Courtesy of Sandi Schneider.)

MILITARY PERSONNEL AT THE FIRST TEE. Chauncey Depew Steele is standing in the back, sixth from the right; Mathilde B. Steele is at the center, above the Steeles' daughter Gloria (cut from the photograph). Many business, political, and religious organizations rented the lodge for conferences. In 1926, the lodge hosted the National Conference on International Problems and Relations, at which a representative of the Philippines warned of a threat to future independence from Japan. This photograph was taken at an unidentified conference. (Courtesy of Sandi Schneider.)

"OFF FOR A MAY-TIME OUTING." After touring over the hills of Westchester in the hotel's new $15,000 motor coach, "society girls" from the Marymount School for Girls in Tarrytown (where this photograph was taken) held their graduation dinner at Briarcliff Lodge. (Courtesy of Sandi Schneider.)

A Costume Ball, 1925. Seen in the front row are, from left to right, Katherine Moran Douglas (with Dorothea Watson behind her), an unidentified person, and Gertrude Watson Law (Henry Law's second wife). Third from the left in the back is Gregory Maue, and to his left is Leila Peacock Maue. Standing to the far right is Henry Law. (Courtesy of the Briarcliff Manor-Scarborough Historical Society.)

A Costume Ball. Chauncey Depew Steele is seen here dressed for a costume ball with his wife, Mathilde Beer Steele. (Courtesy of Sandi Schneider.)

The Great Hall Clock. "The furnishings of this hall express the general tone of the lodge better than any other room. Everything is of the richest, from the celebrated rose vase which the City of Dresden sent as its exhibit to Paris in 1900 to the tall cathedral clock which chimes out the hours besides the entrance, and yet so harmoniously chosen and arranged that there is always the element of comfort, of refinement, and the indescribable something which is called 'home feeling.' " (*Briarcliff Outlook*.) This clock remained inside the lodge right until the King's College closed in 1994. (Courtesy of Sandi Schneider.)

The Great Hall Fireplace. Among the dignitaries who entered Briarcliff Lodge through the Great Hall were Franklin and Eleanor Roosevelt. Eleanor Roosevelt spoke here several times in the early 1930s before the Women's Democratic Club of Mount Pleasant, of which her daughter Anna Roosevelt Dall was chairwoman. In 1930, New York State governor Franklin Roosevelt spoke at the lodge to the Westchester County Bankers Association. (Courtesy of Sandi Schneider.)

The Great Hall Doorway. Beyond the far set of doors was an Italian marble staircase in the 1909 tower extension. (Courtesy of Sandi Schneider.)

THE OAK ROOM. This room was an extension off the east side of the north wing. It served as the apartment for hotel manager Chauncey Depew Steele and his family in the 1920s. The Steele children were all involved in athletics at Briarcliff. Chauncey Steele Jr. excelled at tennis and golf as a teenager. B. Altman designed the interior decoration of the Oak Room in addition to hosting fashion shows at Briarcliff Lodge. (Courtesy of Sandi Schneider.)

THE OAK ROOM. This 35- by 50-foot extension was built in 1909 for Ella Holmes White, who held a long-term lease. White and her traveling companion, Marie G. Young, piano teacher to the children of Pres. Theodore Roosevelt, were survivors of the sinking of the *Titanic* in 1912. (Courtesy of Sandi Schneider.)

THE DINING ROOM. The dining rooms were located at the south end of the building and offered views in three directions. The menu offered fresh dairy, garden, and hatchery produce from the famous Briarcliff Farms. Meals were served on the European and American plans. The tables were covered with Irish linens designed expressly for the lodge. The kitchen was built entirely of marble and was a duplicate of the kitchen in the Manhattan Hotel in New York City. (Courtesy of Sandi Schneider.)

THE STONE DINING ROOM. "The Stone Dining-room, cozily tucked away in the deep woods—a perfect retreat, a haven of coolness and quiet." (Hotel brochure.) The distinctive feature of this room was the floor of six-inch squares of red potters tiles inset with three-foot squares of minor tile in Moravian design. This dining room was built in 1909. Maurice LaCroix was hired as head chef of the lodge in 1923. (Courtesy of Sandi Schneider.)

THE DUTCH KITCHEN. Visitors did not need an overnight reservation to use the lodge dining rooms. Chauncey Depew Steele advertised the lodge as an attractive place to stop for motorists on the Albany Post Road (Route 9) or the newly paved Saw Mill River Road. Dinners on fine-weather Sundays were popular with the "duster and goggles set." From 1909 Briarcliff Lodge was a destination on the Automobile Club of America's Ideal Tour. (Courtesy of Sandi Schneider.)

THE MOOSE HEADS. The two moose heads outside the Great Hall and in the book shop became icons of the lodge over the years. (Courtesy of Sandi Schneider.)

THE VIEW FROM THE TOWER ROOF SOUTHWARD TOWARD NEW YORK CITY. Harmony Hall and the laundry building are visible at bottom, with the Pierson greenhouses at left. The Hudson River winds its way to New York City in the center. "A short trip brings one from the restlessness, noise and dirt of a city that exhausts, to the repose, comfort and ease of a civilization that builds up and inspires." (Hotel brochure.) (Courtesy of Sandi Schneider.)

TENNIS. The 15 clay tennis courts north of the lodge hosted Westchester County championships as well as professional exhibitions. On a cold and windy April 17, 1932, world professional champion Bill Tilden defeated Hans Nusslein, European champion, in a 6-3, 5-7, 6-3 match officiated by New York City mayor Jimmy Walker. Vincent Richards—Davis Cup member, future Olympic champion, and Yonkers, New York, native—played at Briarcliff in 1923. (Courtesy of Sandi Schneider.)

"A TRAINLOAD OF SNOW ARRIVES FOR SKIERS." On January 10, 1924, snow from the Adirondack Mountains arrived at Scarborough for a ski exhibition by the U.S. Olympic team prior to their trip to Chamonix. It was four degrees below freezing, but snow had not fallen here. The *New York Times* called it the first cargo of snow in history. Chauncey D. Steele is the man in the back. Helene W. Beer is at the far left. (Courtesy of Sandi Schneider.)

THE METROPOLITAN MASONS' COUNTRY CLUB CLUBHOUSE. Chauncey D. Steele purchased what had been Walter Law's residence in 1928 and leased it to the Metropolitan Masons, who operated the Briarcliff Lodge Golf Course. The clubhouse contained a boxing arena, bowling alleys, a billiard room, a 5,000-volume library, and a pipe organ installed at a cost of $25,000. In 1929, Chauncey Depew Steele subdivided the land around the house in 51 building lots known as "Kidderminster." (Courtesy of Sandi Schneider.)

A Golfer at the First Tee. Although overnight guests could play at the Briarcliff Lodge golf course, membership in one of the several exclusive athletic clubs allowed special privileges. In 1928, Jerome Brandt, a Mason, and Sol Fink and Herbert Solomon accused the Metropolitan Masons of anti-Semitism for not allowing them to join the country club. The club denied the charges but soon changed its name to the Metropolitan Manor Country Club. (Courtesy of the Briarcliff Manor-Scarborough Historical Society.)

Chauncey Depew Steele (Left) and Gene Sarazen (Center). In December 1922, Steele signed Sarazen, the 21-year-old rising star of the golf world and a Westchester County native, to a two-year contract to be the golf professional. The 1922 U.S. Open and PGA champion signed for approximately $10,000 per year. Sarazen soon found himself at odds with his new employer, who did not want him to play in the 1923 British Open. He was eventually allowed to play. (Courtesy of Sandi Schneider.)

NIGHT GOLF. In October 1928, the Illuminating Engineers Society held their annual meeting at Briarcliff Lodge. They promoted their work to an audience of 10,000 people who came to watch Gene Sarazen play golf under the light of a 400-million-candlepower lamp mounted on a motor truck and numerous other lights and reflectors. Searchlights blazed across the night sky as well. On October 28, the second night of the event, Sarazen (shown here) made a hole in one. (Courtesy of Westchester County Historical Society.)

GOLFERS ON THE COURSE. The golf course was the site of some unfortunate and unusual circumstances. Thomas Larkin, mayor of the city of Yonkers, died of a stroke while standing at the 13th tee on July 25, 1926, during the annual outing of the Yonkers City Club. On August 3, 1931, a Swallow biplane piloted by Jack McCarthy of Rosedale, Long Island, and Douglas Turnbull of Garden City, Long Island, was forced to make an emergency landing near the seventh hole. (Courtesy of Sandi Schneider.)

The Outdoor Pool. Many world records were set at Briarcliff. Johnny Weissmuller swam the 100-meter freestyle in 57 3/5 seconds on July 4, 1928, with the U.S. Olympic team. Olympic champions Helen Meany and Aileen Riggan swam here in 1931. Gertrude Ederle, famous for swimming across the English Channel, swam here throughout the 1920s. With a capacity of six million gallons, the outdoor pool was said to be the largest in the world. (Courtesy of the Briarcliff Manor-Scarborough Historical Society.)

Nighttime Swimming. Evening swimming and dancing were popular with the younger crowd at Briarcliff Lodge. On May 24, 1925, Chauncey Depew Steele, U.S. senators James Wadsworth and Royal Copeland, and Dean Rusby and Professor Kerr from Columbia University placed tobernite, a radioactive ore, in the pool to create a spa that would help relieve "hardening of the arteries, rheumatism and digestive disorders" and other "old age" ailments. (Courtesy of Sandi Schneider.)

Four

EDGEWOOD PARK SCHOOL 1936–1954

In June 1937, Theodore Law, son of Henry Law and grandson of Walter Law, sold the Briarcliff Lodge and 23 acres to the Edgewood Park School, previously located in Greenwich, Connecticut. The Edgecliff Realty Company, a property-management corporation, technically owned the real estate and leased it to the school. In 1937, 101 women graduated during the school's first year at Briarcliff, out of a total enrollment of 278 students. The sale, reportedly valued at $750,000, did not include the 130-acre golf course. Ultimately, that land was to be developed separately.

The Christian, nonsectarian school was founded by Dr. Matthew Reaser. He taught high school–level college-preparatory classes in addition to upper-level "instruction in a wide variety of subjects which will permit a young woman to earn her own livelihood if that be necessary." The school's graduates were "accepted by college without examination." General degrees were granted in addition to degrees in arts, costume design, home economics, interior decoration, journalism, kindergarten, liberal arts, medical assistant, real estate secretarial, secretarial science, and social service. Although there was a high standard of education, Edgewood Park was never recognized as an accredited junior college in New York State.

Matthew Reaser's daughters and their husbands taught classes and helped manage the school during its stay in Briarcliff Manor, including Helen Reaser Temple, academic dean; Harriet Reaser Sowell, registrar and later managing executive; and Gilbert Vance Temple and Shannon Cabell Wallace, directors of business administration. Norman Britton Sowell was school physician, and Agnes Reaser Wallace taught voice instruction.

In August 1954, Theodore Law, who held the mortgage on Briarcliff Lodge, foreclosed on the Edgewood Park School, which defaulted on interest payments by upward of 60 days. Edgewood Park came up with the money after being delivered notice, but a court ruling upheld Law's right to foreclose. The school never reopened.

After Edgewood Park closed, debate quickly ensued within the village of Briarcliff Manor regarding the future of the campus. Village residents protested a plan for a hotel. A group headed by Frank Moroze and Emanuel Shapiro agreed to purchase the 30-acre property from the Edgecliff Realty Corporation in September 1954. They planned to spend as much a $500,000 to improve the property. Twenty-seven residents challenged a zoning variance granting permission to operate a hotel on the lodge grounds. The residents' lawsuit was eventually rejected, based on the fact that the lodge was originally used as a hotel and likely could only operate profitably as such. However, Moroze and Shapiro withdrew their interest because of the delay in the zoning process. Thus came the definitive end of the hostelry business at Briarcliff. The lodge sat empty until the following summer, when it was purchased by the King's College.

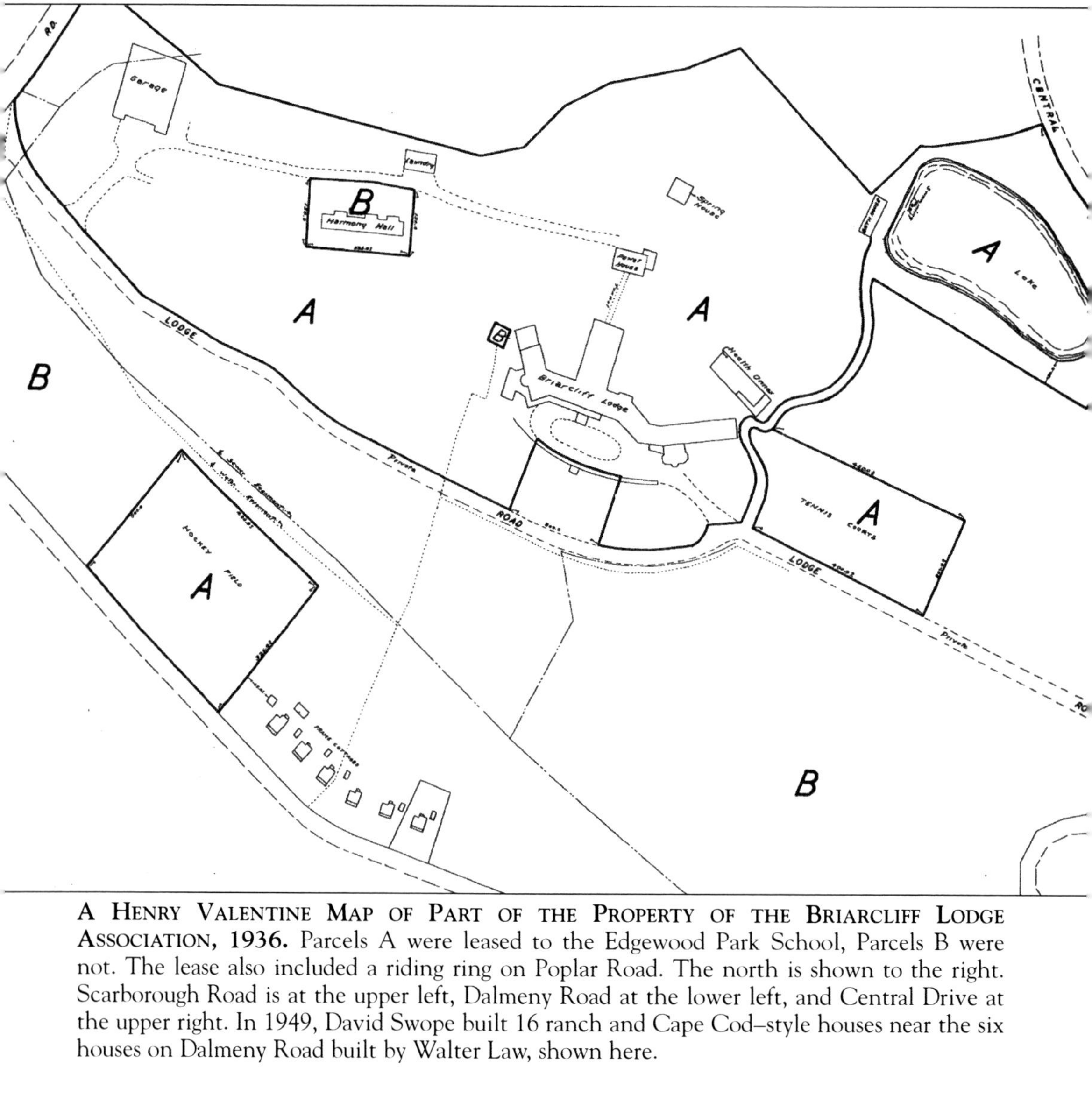

A Henry Valentine Map of Part of the Property of the Briarcliff Lodge Association, 1936. Parcels A were leased to the Edgewood Park School, Parcels B were not. The lease also included a riding ring on Poplar Road. The north is shown to the right. Scarborough Road is at the upper left, Dalmeny Road at the lower left, and Central Drive at the upper right. In 1949, David Swope built 16 ranch and Cape Cod–style houses near the six houses on Dalmeny Road built by Walter Law, shown here.

A PANORAMIC VIEW OF BRIARCLIFF LODGE. The Edgewood Park Junior College held its first graduation in Greenwich, Connecticut, in 1933, when 14 students were awarded diplomas. The school signed a 10-year lease to use the Edgewood Inn in 1932 and successfully defended a $100,000 lawsuit claiming breach of contract when the school moved to Briarcliff Manor.

A BRIARCLIFF LODGE ADVERTISEMENT, 1939. The hotel operated through one last summer in 1939. John W. Greene, managing director, and Carter L. Gardner, resident manager, oversaw the hotel operations during this time. The most famous resort ever built in the Hudson Valley, the Catskill Mountain House, closed its doors for good following the 1942 season.

DR. AND MRS. MATTHEW HOWELL REASER, 1946. Born in Leavenworth, Kansas, Matthew Howell Reaser received his doctorate from Westminster College in Fulton, Missouri. A proponent of higher education for women, he had previously been president at Lindenwood College and later Wilson College before founding the Beechwood School in Jenkintown, Pennsylvania, in 1912.

THE REASER RESIDENCE, CHILMARK PARK, 1939. The Reasers lived in this house on Noel Drive in the village of Ossining. They later lived on Lodge Road, where Matthew Reaser died on February 17, 1948, at the age of 85. The Noel Drive house still stands. It is a private residence.

Edgewood Park, 1939. This page from the 1939 yearbook shows a variety of scenes from the campus and from the class trips to the World's Fair in Queens, New York. Eileen O'Connor-Weber, longtime Briarcliff Manor resident and graduate of Edgewood Park, recalled that tuition for one year, including a class trip to Bermuda, cost $870 a year in the 1930s.

East Front, North Wing, 1937. "Briarcliff Lodge, home of Edgewood Park for Young Women, is one of the most beautiful and adequate properties for education use in the country." (Hotel brochure.) (Photograph from Edgewood Park yearbook.)

The West Front of the Lodge, Showing Foo Dogs. The grounds and landscape of the Edgewood Park School remained unchanged from the hotel era. The school constructed no new buildings on the campus. (Photograph by Edward Thayer Monroe, courtesy of the King's College)

The Merchandising Club, 1946. The south end of the lodge originally featured a columned portico adjacent to the outdoor pergola. This section was later enclosed by the King's College. (Photograph from Edgewood Park yearbook.)

The Golf Club, 1939. This view shows Dalmeny Road in the background. Athletics were popular at Edgewood Park. Sports included badminton, tennis, horseback riding, skiing, field hockey, and ice-skating. The riding club used the stables at Sleepy Hollow Country Club. (Photograph from Edgewood Park yearbook.)

THE LOBBY, 1946. Edgewood Park maintained Briarcliff's interior as the hotel did before. Hotel furnishings and $25,000 worth of paintings and etchings remained in the lodge with the Edgewood Park School. (Photograph from Edgewood Park yearbook.)

THE DIRECTORS, 1953. The directors pose in front of the decorative Oak Room fireplace mantel. The room was Edgewood Park's library. (Photograph from Edgewood Park yearbook.)

THE KINDERGARTEN CLUB, 1939. The room shown here was formerly the library of the Briarcliff Lodge. It later became the president's office of the King's College. (Photograph from Edgewood Park yearbook.)

THE MEDICAL ASSISTANTS ASSOCIATION, 1946. A typical classroom scene at the Briarcliff campus is shown here. The members of the Medical Assistants Association took rigorous courses and were highly sought after by doctors. They received practical training at the nearby Grasslands Hospital. (Photograph from Edgewood Park yearbook.)

THE CLASS OF 1953. The second-to-last class to graduate Edgewood Park School poses in the lobby. (Photograph by Edward Thayer Monroe.)

Five

The King's College 1955–1994

The King's College was founded in 1938 in Belmar, New Jersey, by Percy Crawford and the Young People's Association for the Propagation of the Gospel. Sixty-seven students enrolled in the school, situated on a 90-acre estate once used by Gulielmo Marconi for wireless experiments. This private coeducational Christian liberal arts school was modeled after Wheaton College in Illinois, Crawford's alma mater. Forced to raise $500,000 for an endowment necessary for accreditation in New Jersey, the school chose instead to find a new home.

In 1941, the King's College purchased a c. 1846 estate in New Castle, Delaware, known as Lexington, which it would make home for the next 14 years. During World War II, enrollment decreased but went up following the war, reaching 260 students by 1950, one year after it was approved as a degree-granting institution. However, within a few years, the surrounding lands were acquired by the Tidewater Associated Oil Company for purposes of building an oil refinery. With this news came another enrollment decrease, and the King's College again was forced to find a new home. In 1955, the school purchased 52 acres in Briarcliff Manor for $380,000.

Enrollment at Briarcliff Manor started at 300 and steadily increased. The school immediately set about expanding its facilities. The neighboring Braeview mansion was acquired as the president's home, and off-campus faculty housing was also purchased. A new gymnasium, Squire Hall, was completed in 1959 after two years of work. Briarcliff Lodge itself received updated electric and heating systems by 1957. Percy Crawford died in 1960, and Dr. Robert A. Cook continued campus improvements after being named president in 1962. Under Cook's leadership, the library expanded, a new dormitory and a new science building were built, and additional properties were acquired.

The Cook years are fondly remembered by alumni but have also been pointed to as the beginning of the decline of Briarcliff Lodge. Deferred maintenance on the aging buildings had been noted, and the village board also opposed expansion plans in the 1970s, making the school less attractive to prospective students. Zoning laws limited what could be built and where, as new buildings could not be erected near adjacent properties. In 1985, after Cook retired, Dr. Friedhelm K. Radant was brought in to stabilize the school.

Radant tried to upgrade the Briarcliff campus, but it soon became apparent that a move was necessary in order for the King's College to survive. Enrollment also declined sharply, to just 170 students in the fall of 1994, after peaking at over 870 students in 1979–1980. In 1991, the college purchased 168 acres in Orange County, New York, from Blue Lake Properties for $12 million. The school took title to the new campus despite paying down a minimal amount. However, the delayed sale of the Briarcliff property to finance the new purchase (see chapter 6) nearly destroyed the King's College. As enrollment bottomed out and teachers (unsure of their future) left, the state education department stripped the school of its accreditation and ordered it to close on December 31, 1994.

After the Briarcliff campus closed, the school sought to sell the property and use the funds to erase debt and open the new campus. In what was described by a federal judge as a "miracle," the college successfully staved off a mortgage foreclosure attempt by Lehman Brothers, holders of the mortgage on the Briarcliff campus. Radant raised $5 million in 1997 to pay off debt, and the school survived by trading the Briarcliff campus to Blue Lake Properties for the Orange County site. In 1997, the King's College merged with Campus Crusade for Christ, led by Bill Bright. Blue Lake Properties assumed ownership of the Briarcliff campus at this time. The school opened a new campus in the Empire State Building in New York City in 1999 after merging with Northeastern Bible College. In May 2004, the board of the King's College voted to sell the Orange County campus and hire a real estate firm to assess the opportunity for a campus in New York City.

BRIARCLIFF LODGE. The King's College continued its tradition of residing in historic buildings when it moved to Briarcliff Manor. In the 1950s, school brochures were titled, tongue-in-cheek, "A Moving Story." (Courtesy of the Westchester County Historical Society.)

THE BRIARCLIFF MANOR RAILROAD STATION. The last passenger train on the Putnam Division ran on May 29, 1958, and the section of track was removed from here in 1963. The village purchased the station and surrounding acre for $10,000 and made it the first permanent home for the library, which opened there on January 20, 1959. Interior renovations were designed by village resident William Sharman. (Courtesy of the Westchester County Historical Society.)

Briarcliff Manor, Aerial View. This mid-20th-century view of Briarcliff Manor shows the campus acquired by the King's College. The lodge and pond are shown to the left of the center

of the image, Briar Hall Country Club is at the right, and Pleasantville Road cuts across the top-right corner. (Courtesy of the King's College.)

PERCY CRAWFORD AND THE BOARD OF TRUSTEES, C. 1956. Percy Crawford (seated, right) and his wife, Ruth, traveled the East Coast in the 1930s, holding gospel services aimed at young people. Pioneers of radio and television evangelism, they founded the Pinebrook Bible Conference summer camp in Pennsylvania. Crawford is credited with being the first televangelist. He taught Bible classes and was president until 1960, when he died at age 58.

This photograph shows Crawford with board members Charles Hans Evans (seated, left), a teacher who later served as interim president; Alex Dunlap (seated, center); and Dave Wright (standing, far left). (Courtesy of the King's College.)

WILLIAM JELLEY III. In 1947, businessman William Jelley was appointed executive vice president to manage finances, to hire and appoint, and to report to the board of trustees of the King's College. His role was important in bringing the school to Briarcliff, as Crawford was president in name only and taught a single freshman class each week. (Courtesy of Ed and Ginger Kuhlman.)

ROBERT A. AND COREEN NILSEN COOK. Dr. Robert A. Cook's term began in March 1962. Previously he served as vice president of Scripture Press Foundation and president of Youth for Christ International. Cook launched *The King's Hour* radio program, which eventually broadcast on over 65 stations daily. (Courtesy of the King's College.)

The Main Facade. The King's College was chartered by the New York State Board of Regents in 1960 and accredited by the Middle States Association in 1967. The curriculum was reformed at this time, and certificates were issued in elementary education, physical education, and music education. (Courtesy of the King's College.)

A Landscape. In addition to preserving the historic buildings of the Briarcliff Lodge resort, the King's College maintained the general landscape design of the campus, including architectural elements such as Walter Law's Japanese lanterns. (Photograph by Hank Winters, courtesy of the King's College.)

The First Library Expansion. The King's College made several alterations to the lodge, including the construction of a small library wing off the south end of the original hotel dining room in 1966 and 1967. (Photograph by Hank Winters, courtesy of the King's College.)

The Library, c. 1978–1982. The library is shown here before it was enlarged in the 1980s. (Photograph by Tim Rice.)

BRIARCLIFF LODGE, FROM THE BASEBALL DIAMOND, C. 1982–1983. The tower wing, at the center, was the men's dormitory. This view shows it in its original appearance before the modern staircase was added on by the King's College. The steam plant is visible below the lodge. The baseball diamond was added in 1978, along with a new track, tennis courts, and a soccer field. The village replaced the original water tower with a new one, at the right, in the early 1960s. (Courtesy of the King's College.)

THE MEN'S DORMITORY. Construction occurred during the 1983–1984 school year. A new staircase was added at the west end of the building, replacing a metal fire escape, and the interior was completely gutted and rebuilt with modern dorm rooms. This wing originally contained 72 bedrooms and 41 baths. Work done in 1978 included installation of new windows to retain heat and save money on fuel consumption. (Courtesy of the King's College.)

THE MEN'S DORMITORY. The men's dorm is shown here from the south, with the new library expansion from the early 1980s also visible at the right. (Courtesy of the King's College.)

THE ROOF GABLE WINDOWS, C. 1983–1984. The steeply pitched gable roof and dormer windows created diverse interior spaces on the fourth floor. (Courtesy of the King's College.)

THE MIRROR ROOM. The King's College converted the Mirror Room into a cafeteria, although it still continued to host parties on the scale of the earlier hotel days. (Courtesy of the King's College.)

THE LIBRARY. At the southern end of the lodge was the library, formerly the dining room of the hotel. Just beyond the windows at the rear was the open-air pergola. Daily life for students at the King's College reflected the religious values of the school. Students were required to sign a pledge not to drink, use tobacco, attend movies or the theater, or to dance. (Photograph by William A. Painter, courtesy of the King's College.)

THE BALLROOM. The ballroom hosted Sunday chapel services and classes. (Photograph by William A. Painter, courtesy of the King's College.)

THE TILED FIREPLACE MANTEL IN THE LOBBY. Architectural ornamentation and detailing was preserved by the King's College. Although new chairs, carpets, and some light fixtures were installed in the 1950s and 1960s, the historic fabric of the building remained as Walter Law had built it. Many original furnishings remained as well. (Courtesy of the King's College.)

THE WOMEN'S DORMITORY, C. MID-1950S. The second, third, and fourth floors of Briarcliff Lodge served as women's dorms. These rooms were originally furnished in mahogany and designed after styles of the early 1800s. All bedrooms faced outward; there were no inside rooms. The primary bedrooms had open fireplaces. When Briarcliff Lodge opened in 1902, long-distance telephones were installed in each bedroom. A hotel brochure claimed that Briarcliff Lodge was one of the first hotels in or near New York to provide that service. (Courtesy of the King's College.)

DR. ROBERT A. COOK WITH PHONEATHON CALLERS, FALL 1983. The grandfather clock on the staircase landing in the main lobby is another enduring symbol of the lodge for many alumni of the King's College. When the school moved to the Empire State Building in 1999, a new grandfather clock was purchased and placed in the lobby of the 15th floor. (Photograph by Michael Ortiz, courtesy of the King's College.)

HOMECOMING, 1990. Alumni pose in front of the fieldstone fireplace in the lobby. (Courtesy of the King's College.)

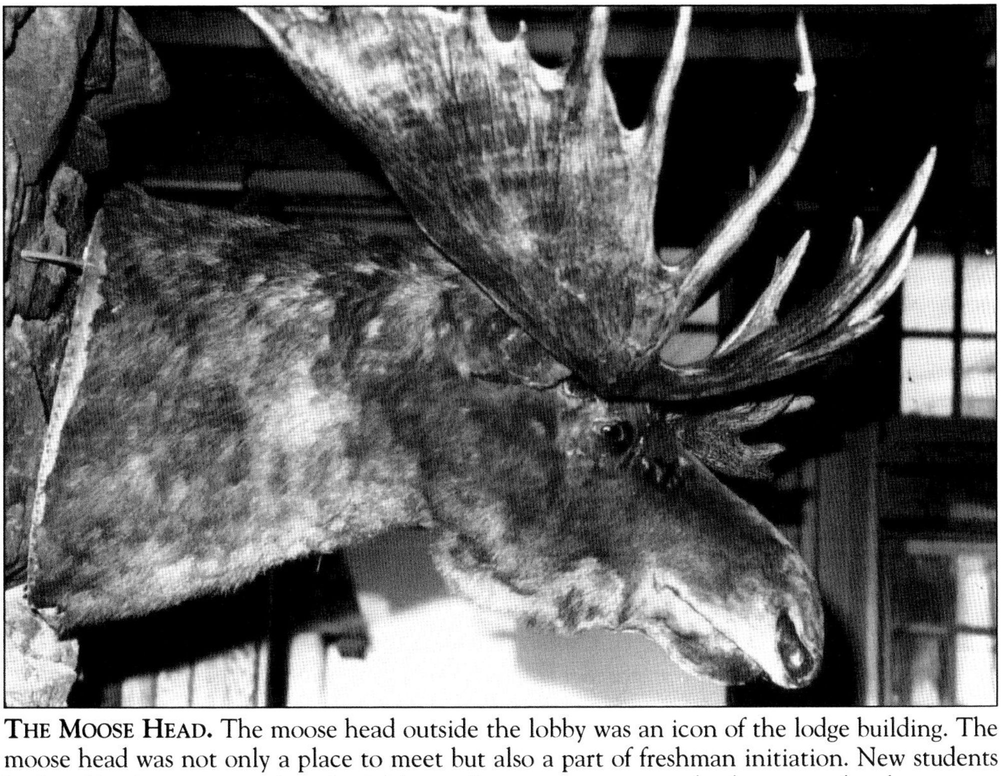

THE MOOSE HEAD. The moose head outside the lobby was an icon of the lodge building. The moose head was not only a place to meet but also a part of freshman initiation. New students had to kiss it at some point. A visiting college soccer team stole the moose head one year. (Courtesy of the King's College.)

The Student Life Building. The former amusement building was first used by the college as the science building. With its indoor swimming pool and other recreational facilities, it became the Student Life Building in 1980. (Courtesy of the King's College.)

Lodge Pond. The famous outdoor swimming pool became a pond, and the swimming pool building and diving board were demolished. The school constructed a track and playing field adjacent to the pond. (Courtesy of the King's College.)

BRAEVIEW. The King's College acquired the Braeview mansion on Central Drive for the residence of the college president. The house was built by George McNeir, an associate of Walter Law and the director and secretary of W&J Sloane. (Courtesy of the Briarcliff Manor-Scarborough Historical Society.)

THE CASTLE, C. 1978–1982. The college purchased Walter Law's mansion in April 1970. For the previous five years, it was owned by Catholics for Latin America, which trained volunteers to help the poor in Latin America. The 30-room mansion contained a 30-bed men's dormitory, a staff apartment, student lounges, and recreation rooms. The dorm closed in the late 1980s and was sold in 1993, again becoming a private home. (Photograph by Tim Rice.)

MILLER CIRCLE. Construction began in August 1968, and the 200-bed women's dormitory opened in the fall of 1970. The building honored William A. Miller, a 20-year member of the board of trustees and its chair for 12 years. (Courtesy of the King's College.)

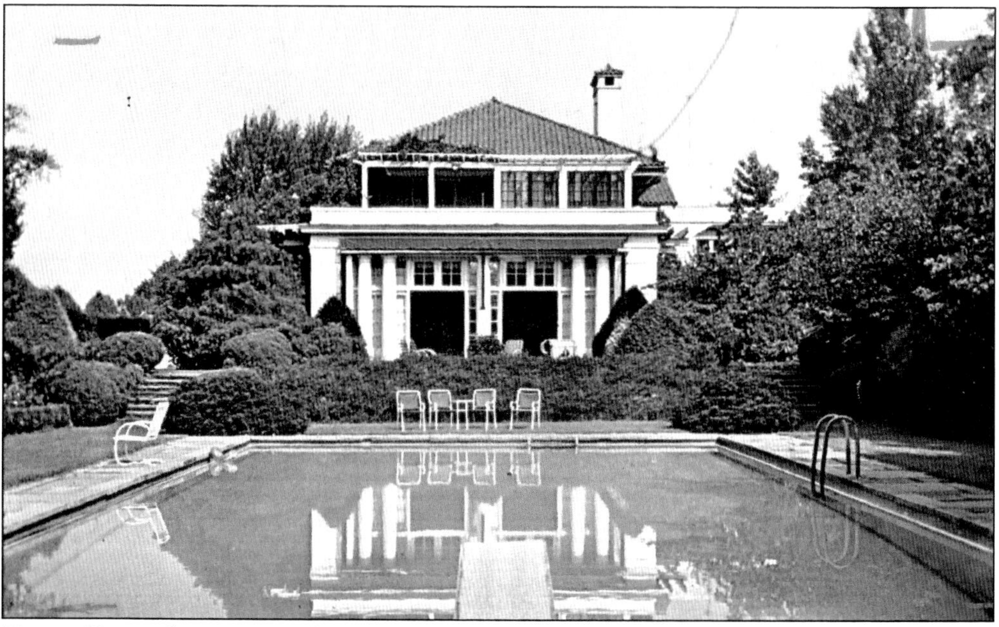

TARRY HILL. The King's College purchased the Tarry Hill Swim and Tennis Club on Cedar Lane in Ossining in 1964 for use as a dormitory. A shuttle bus brought students to and from the main campus. The King's College sold Tarry Hill in the 1980s. Faculty housing in Tarrytown and Briarcliff Manor were sold in the early 1990s. Tarry Hill has been demolished, but its carriage house survives. (Courtesy of the King's College.)

THE DEDICATION CEREMONY, OCTOBER 13, 1979. The dedication of the new academic-science building in honor of Dr. Rober A. Cook was not announced until the ceremony. (Courtesy of the King's College.)

THE COOK BUILDING, C. 1982–1983. The Robert A. Cook Academic-Science Building contained classrooms and science laboratories, a lecture hall, and a greenhouse. (Courtesy of the King's College.)

HARMONY HALL DEMOLITION. This early-1900s building was originally used as worker's quarters for Briarcliff Farms employees. The King's College used it for classrooms and staff housing. It was demolished in the fall of 1979 shortly after the dedication for the new science building, which was built on the adjacent plot. (Courtesy of the King's College.)

THE MUSIC BUILDING. This two-story structure stood opposite Harmony Hall and, later, the Robert A. Cook Academic-Science Building, which is seen at the right in this photograph from the 1982–1983 school year. This building was constructed in 1909 as a laundry for Briarcliff Lodge. (Courtesy of the King's College.)

A SOCCER GAME, HOMECOMING, 1983. Athletics were an important part of campus life for students of the college, just as athletics were integral to the operation of the lodge as a resort 60 years earlier. However, athletic events were later strongly opposed by some neighbors of the campus, who sought to prevent further activities of this type and size from occurring again on the property. (Courtesy of the King's College.)

GRADUATION, 1988. Dr. Friedhelm K. Radant shares a happy moment with graduating students. The first graduation from the Empire State Building campus occurred in 2002. In 2004, the school counted 257 students, more than there were when the school left Briarcliff Manor. (Courtesy of the King's College.)

A Fish-Eye View of Briarcliff Lodge. This unique view of Briarcliff Lodge captures the harmony of the natural landscape with the distinguished aesthetics of the lodge. The spirit of the person who created this image is evidenced by the photographer's shadow at the lower right. (Courtesy of the King's College.)

Six

Abandoned 1995–2003

The closing of the King's College in December 1994 ultimately proved to be the end of Briarcliff Lodge, although there soon developed plans that would have seen the lodge regain its earlier splendor. In the early 1990s, the college succeeded in selling several adjacent houses and parcels, whittling down the size of the 84-acre campus. In 1992, Tara Circle, a nonprofit educational institution dedicated to preserving and promoting Irish culture and history entered into agreement with the King's College to purchase the core 57 acres for $14 million, even though local real estate agencies estimated the actual value of the land to be closer to $5 million. The sale of the campus would have allowed the college to complete its move to the new campus in Orange County.

Tara Circle sought to build "the largest cultural center outside of Dublin" in Briarcliff. The lodge was to be converted into a genealogy and research library, and a museum for Irish artists. Plans for the campus included a 350-person-capacity banquet hall, a 100-person dining hall, and a 40-person lounge. Such limits were put in place by a temporary special-use zoning permit granted by the village of Briarcliff Manor. The permit also limited Gaelic Athletic Association football matches to women's and junior men's events, with bleacher seating for 300 people.

Tara Circle's plan was controversial within the village, and many residents rallied against the granting of the special-use permit. Fearing traffic, noise, and congestion, a group calling itself Residents for the Future of Briarcliff Manor launched a lawsuit to dismiss the permit. The suit was rejected in the state supreme court in White Plains in 1996, and an appeal by the residents group and a new village board was also turned down in 1997.

The saga took its toll on Tara Circle, which claimed anti-Irish bias by the village of Briarcliff Manor. In April 1996, a new mayor and two new trustees, all of whom opposed Tara Circle, were elected. The new board created a new special-use permit provision that had the effect of deterring investors from joining Tara Circle. Tara Circle missed a mortgage payment and began to look elsewhere for a new site. Tara Circle also filed a $250 million lawsuit of its own alleging that anti-Irish hostility prevented it from taking over the campus. The suit was rejected in 1999 by the Federal Appeals Court in Manhattan, citing the issuance of the special-use permit by the village as an act by itself that did not hinder the acquisition of the property by Tara Circle. Legalities aside, the issue deeply divided the residents of Briarcliff Manor, and the words of some residents at village meetings inspired letters of protest from across the country in favor of Tara Circle.

Blue Lake Properties, based in Rockland County, New York, took title to the campus in December 1997 and, in 1998, contracted to sell the property to Barrington Venture, an Illinois-based developer. Barrington Venture proposed a retirement community, the Garlands at Briarcliff, consisting of 500 independent-living and assisted-care units, and a 1,000-space underground parking facility. Unlike Tara Circle, Barrington Venture planned to demolish all existing buildings on the property. As plans were debated, Briarcliff Lodge and the other buildings sat unused and unprotected. Briarcliff Lodge had no security guard to watch over it. Vandals broke windows, and a stone fireplace mantel was stolen.

Architect Michael Molinelli toured Briarcliff Lodge in 2003 and proposed that the old hotel could indeed be saved and adaptively reused. The total cost of Barrington Venture's plan was approximately $150 million, and Molinelli suggested that saving the lodge, as opposed to tearing down and building anew, would cost only an additional 4.3 percent. Barrington Venture, however, felt that the design of the lodge was not workable. In the spring of 2003, Barrington Venture's permit to develop the Garlands at Briarcliff was granted, and demolition of existing buildings was set to begin in the fall.

THE EAST FACADE, FEBRUARY 10, 2000. The author, Michael Molinelli, and others raised awareness about Briarcliff Lodge in an effort to save the building. Some residents, including the Briarcliff Manor Scarborough Historical Society, supported Molinelli's findings.

The North Wing, East Front, September 5, 2000. Briarcliff Lodge sat abandoned but not forgotten. Articles appeared in the *New York Times*, the *Journal News* (a local newspaper), and *Preservation* magazine concerning the abandoned property. Robert Worth of the *New York Times* wrote, "From the outside, the lodge looks like a campus in the aftermath of a sudden epidemic. Pamphlets advertising student activity groups and alumni meetings drift in the breeze on the empty walkways. A few battered bikes are still locked to stands."

Dormer Windows, February 10, 2000. Although no one ever tried to list Briarcliff Lodge on any historic register, the building met several criteria for listing on the National Register of Historic Places, including that it be at least 50 years old, that its architectural integrity remain intact, and that it be significant. The building's significance can be national, statewide, or local, and can be defined by association with significant persons or architectural significance.

THE PORTE COCHERE, FEBRUARY 10, 2000. After its abandonment, Briarcliff Lodge fell victim to vandalism.

THE VERANDA, MAY 28, 2000. Briarcliff Lodge was still fit for restoration or adaptive reuse. In Kingston, New York, for example, the city chose to restore city hall, which had been abandoned for 28 years, much longer than Briarcliff Lodge sat empty. Kingston's landmark office reopened in 2000, while the destruction of Briarcliff Lodge was planned.

THE 1907 WING FROM THE TOWER, APRIL 8, 2000. Despite several years of abandonment, electrical and phone service still worked in the lodge. "The building was still fully powered until this fall (1999) as well, the servers running up on the roof of the men's dorms were kept running as well for some unknown reason, in addition on the north wing upper floors also had lights still on, was VERY spooky at night as well," stated Ian Gall.

THE 1907 WING, MAY 28, 2000. By the time this photograph was taken, the grounds were overgrown, but roadways and walkways were maintained.

THE 1902 WING, WEST FRONT, FEBRUARY 17, 2000. Because windows were not boarded up, they were broken by vandals or were left open. Such exposure to the weather can speed up the process of decay.

THE TILED FIREPLACE MANTEL, THE GREAT HALL, MAY 28, 2000. The abandoned Briarcliff Lodge was the subject of many urban legends regarding haunting and other unusual activities. An alumnus of the King's College stated that "many, many, many people have seen and heard parties going on in the ballroom. Sometimes the faint smell of alcohol would traipse up the stairs of the men's dormitories. As you know, King's was a dry college. The piano would play at night . . . and lights would go on in the attics and other rooms where no one was living, especially in the summer."

THE STONE FIREPLACE, THE GREAT HALL, MAY 28, 2000. Guests entering Briarcliff Lodge under the porte cochere came into the large central hall. "[Its] most striking feature is the great fireplace and chimney of rough local stone—one of those genial old fireplaces whose red-tiled hearth suggest hospitable welcome." (*Briarcliff Outlook.*)

THE OAK ROOM, FEBRUARY 10, 2000. The fireplace mantel here was stolen from the lodge in late 1999. One inscription on the mantel read, "Sit with me by the homestead hearth and stretch the hands of memory forth to warm them by the woodfires ember." Another inscription read, "Tv Ne Cede Malis Sed Contra Avdentoir Ito." The verse, by Virgil (*The Aeneid*), translates roughly to "Do not give in to evil, but proceed ever more boldly against it."

A WALL COVERING, FEBRUARY 4, 2001. This early-20th-century cloth wall covering survived in a first-floor room.

A CHANDELIER. Quite a few relics of the lodge miraculously survived many years of abandonment, such as this first-floor chandelier. The hanging bronze electric lights provided "a mellow glow which is artistic and yet thoroughly general and home-like." (Photograph by Karl Xydexx Jorgensen.)

THE DUTCH KITCHEN, FEBRUARY 4, 2001. The Dutch Kitchen (shown here) was one of two unique rooms of the lodge. The other was the Japanese Tea Room at the south end of the second floor. It was decorated with imported bamboo and exquisite carved panels and opened to a large balcony. The wine steward's closet was located at the north end of the Dutch Kitchen behind sliding batten doors.

THE STONE DINING ROOM, SEPTEMBER 7, 2000. "Just beyond the main lobby to the left was the dining room with detailed corbelled wood columns spreading out like trees to the coffered ceiling. Flat arched windows of leaded glass looked south and west towards the Hudson River," stated Michael Molinelli.

THE STAIRWAY LANDING, LOOKING TOWARD THE GREAT HALL, AUGUST 8, 2000. The Italian marble staircase at the east end of the 1909 tower extension led down to the Mirror Room from the Great Hall and the ballroom.

THE STAIRWAY LANDING, LOOKING TOWARD THE BALLROOM, MAY 28, 2000. A former staff member of the King's College Nightwatch (security) stated, "One night around 3 a.m. in the morning we were patrolling through the basement getting the keys there with the watch clock when we heard a noise. Nothing in particular or attainable but noise. We went further down the hall where it comes out by the elevator and what was the cafeteria and we stopped and listened to people laughing, swing music, etc. We shuddered . . . didn't know what to think. We began running upstairs to investigate. Once we reached the second landing on the stairs we were pushed back to the wall and a huge beam of light came and circled down the stairway and into the basement foyer and down the basement hall."

A COLUMN CAPITAL, BALLROOM, MAY 28, 2000. The lodge did have a history that was not always happy and celebratory. In the early-morning hours of December 26, 1925, Alfred Fraser, a 28-year-old bellboy, committed suicide while jazz orchestras played for Christmas revelers. Despondent over a broken love affair, Fraser jumped from a porch roof outside the ballroom, and his body was later found in a flowerbed, as reported in the *New York Times*.

THE MIRROR ROOM, FEBRUARY 4, 2001. A late afternoon in winter provided an opportunity for a spectacular display of reflected rays of brilliant sunlight in the Mirror Room.

THE DINING ROOM, FEBRUARY 4, 2001. This part of the building housed library stacks for the King's College. A former staff member of the King's College Nightwatch (security) stated, "The most activity was in the library and in the deepest part of the basement. The library lights would go on and off as they pleased. Books would be stacked and arranged strangely on the tables. (This would be between tours, 50 minutes apart.)"

THE KITCHEN, FEBRUARY 4, 2001. "The Formal Lounge always smelled like freshly baked bread cooking from Mama and Papa Short in the kitchen. It was a very homelike atmosphere," stated Richard Smiraldi. The fireproof kitchen was built for the hotel with white vitreous (nonabsorbent) tiles and plate glass-lined refrigerators so that the meats would not have to come in contact with ice. Also, originally located in the basement were the billiard room, barbershop, telephone room, and the mechanical plant.

THE SECOND-FLOOR BALUSTRADE, FEBRUARY 10, 2000. This wooden stair railing was stolen in 2000.

THE SECOND-FLOOR HALLWAY, FEBRUARY 10, 2000. In 1998, a nonprofit organization in New York City was given authorization to enter Briarcliff Lodge and claim what could be of use. Over several months, the group hauled out trucks full of equipment. This included bunk beds, springs, desks, cabinets, and even mattresses. A salvage company removed more furniture in early 2000.

A SECOND-FLOOR WOMEN'S DORMITORY ROOM, FEBRUARY 10, 2000. On the second and third floors, most bathrooms were connected to two dorm rooms, one larger room and one smaller room. The large rooms housed four women and the small rooms two. The fourth floor featured communal bathrooms with individual stalls, allowing for slightly more privacy.

A WOMEN'S DORMITORY ROOM. A former staff member of the King's College Nightwatch (security) stated, "Once there was a call from the 3rd floor of a strange man walking the hallways. This same man would reappear every so often in the same clothes and almost identical reports from different girls. He was always well dressed, fifty-ish and always ignored when someone tried to holler to him. My last year there I believe the supervisor recorded 22 sightings/reports of this man." (Photograph by Karl Xydexx Jorgensen.)

A THIRD-FLOOR WOMEN'S DORMITORY ROOM, FEBRUARY 4, 2001. The device at the right below the window is a type of fire escape composed of flexible steel cables wound on a reel that could be unfurled and let down from the window. The Harris portable fire escape was advertised in the *Briarcliff Outlook* in the early 1900s. The 1909 tower extension is visible through the windows.

A THIRD-FLOOR BATHROOM, FEBRUARY 10, 2000. The bathrooms consisted of solid porcelain baths and basins and, in the early 20th century, were equal to those in the most expensive private dwellings. Public bathrooms were found at the south end of the second and third floors.

THE SEVENTH FLOOR OF THE TOWER, AUGUST 8, 2000. Most of the vandalism at Briarcliff Lodge was limited to superficial damage, such as broken windows and spray paint. Modern sheetrock walls in the renovated tower extension were damaged far more easily than the original lodge walls.

A ROOFTOP VIEW OF THE HUDSON RIVER, JULY 1, 2000. Although dirigibles never moored off the roof of the tower, it was found to be a popular spot for sunbathers. From the roof, one could easily view the skyscrapers of Manhattan, including the Empire State Building and the World Trade Center. Walter Law's mansion is seen at the left of the center of the image.

May 14, 1993

in tranquil reflection

Hello. We, Heidi Grovatt and Sherri Young, have had many great memories in this room. We lived here together from FA1990 to Sp. 1992. We were students at The King's College. Tomorrow Heidi will graduate with a BA Psychology, next year Sherri will graduate with a BS in Music education (if the school survives). Next year they're closing this wing, so no one will be living here. The next year the school is supposed to move to the Sterling Forrest campus.

This room, though many have lived here in the last 3 years, has always been favored as the best. With the firescape, kitchenette, and the interesting dividing wall has made it unique.

But the best thing that has happened in this room is the friendship that has grown between us all, especially Heidi (Diana) and Sherri (Anne). We will always look back to The King's College and Rm 456 with a happy tear of good memories.

Sherri Young & Heidi Grovatt

A Letter Found in Room 456. Written by Heidi Grovatt and Sherri Young, this letter was found inside the lodge eight years after it was written and seven years after the lodge was abandoned. Another letter and other personal effects dating to the hotel era were also found inside the abandoned lodge. (Courtesy of Karl Xydexx Jorgensen.)

BRIARCLIFF LODGE AND THE AMUSEMENT BUILDING, NOVEMBER 18, 2000. The lodge and amusement building show two very different styles of architecture that were both popular *c.* 1900.

THE 1909 TOWER AND STEAM PLANT, FROM THE TRACK, MAY 28, 2000. Activity continued to flourish on the abandoned campus. Village residents took to using the old college track for walking and running. People would frequently fish in the pond as well. Turkeys and hawks were commonly seen on the property. Someone even left food and water for a small cat living at the steam plant.

SQUIRE HALL, FEBRUARY 17, 2000. Squire Hall, the gymnasium built by the King's College, hosted athletic events as well and graduation ceremonies. The steps leading from Squire Hall to Briarcliff Lodge were known to King's College students as "the chapel steps," after daily services were moved to the gym.

SQUIRE HALL'S INTERIOR, MAY 28, 2000. Until the hoops were removed, it was known that some people still used the abandoned gym to play basketball.

THE FIRST TEE, NOVEMBER 10, 2000. For two years, a giant police dog named Thor, owned by Olney B. Mairs, retrieved wayward golf balls. On September 30, 1926, Thor chased an errant ball and was hit by a car coming up the Lodge Drive below the first tee. When he was picked up, Thor dropped the ball at the caddy master's feet and gave one last wag of his tail as the huddled golfers grieved, as reported in the *New York Times*.

THE COOK BUILDING, SEPTEMBER 5, 2000. Even after several years of abandonment, the Cook building had not been completely emptied. Scientific equipment and machines, glassware and laboratory materials, and cabinets full of photographic slides remained. This view shows the hallway between the greenhouse and the lecture hall.

THE LAUNDRY BUILDING, OCTOBER 1, 2000. After a small fire at the laundry building on September 30, 2000, the village board mandated that a security team be assembled to guard the property. This building was demolished in the summer of 2002. The Briarcliff Garage had been demolished in the winter of 1999–2000.

MILLER CIRCLE, SEPTEMBER 5, 2000. It was perhaps most strange to see Miller Circle and the Cook building, two relatively new structures, in a state of abandonment.

THE PORTE COCHERE, JUNE 16, 2003. In the spring of 2003, the porte cochere, a freestanding structure, collapsed.

Seven

FIRE
SEPTEMBER 20, 2003

The pager beeped and sputtered just before any hint of dawn. "To all fire department personnel: Smoke seen from King's College by the water tower." It was happening—the thing we dreaded and trained for, for many years.

When Rescue 37 was on the scene, we opened the door on the rear, and the compartment was flooded with orange light. I could see the skeletal wood timbers of the building darkly charred through, the soaring flames reaching toward the top of the water tower. The rafters and beams clung desperately to the six brick chimneys before they thundered consent and fell to the basement. The old building was completely engulfed. The clear sky was just turning from navy blue to azure right behind it. It was Saturday, September 20, 2003, and the Briarcliff Lodge was burning.

When we heard the call for the "old King's College," we knew what we were up against. It was our big one. The oldest section of the lodge was heavy timber construction, which is about 70,000 square feet of fire-load spread over four stories. The 1907 addition was a concrete structure, but it had plenty of interior wood paneling to burn. The 1909 seven-story tower was also fire-resistant construction. As there was no electricity in the building to spark anything, the sprinkler system and alarm systems had not been functioning for many years. Any smaller fire could smolder for hours and burst into flames before anyone would know about it. If the winds had been blowing like the day before (the aftermath of the periphery of tropical storm Isabel), the fire could have been swept around the building, igniting nearby trees and homes.

Our aerial ladder was in place near the 1907 addition, outside the collapse zone of the stucco, brick, and stone facade. I put on my ladder belt and ascended to the top that extended 75 feet in the air. From that elevated perch, as the smoke began to dissipate, I could see other streams coming from the firefighters on the west side of the building. Their crews hauled multiple five-inch lines from the bottom of a 50-foot-tall steep incline. I could see both valleys that define Briarcliff, from the hill of the lodge to the east and to the Hudson River. I wondered if our village would ever see such a glory again as was Walter William Law's grand old dame, the Briarcliff Lodge.

By the early afternoon, the major fire had been knocked down. I was in one of the crews that went inside the still standing 1907 addition to search for any smoldering fires. Inside, the atmosphere was eerily calm, like a wake. Smoke moved through the halls, dancing around the sunlight, streaming in from glassless windows. The rhythm of me breathing through my mask was the only sound I heard. Small fires burned innocuously in corners of the wood paneling as if they knew they would be ignored for a while.

If this was the funeral pyre for the grand old dame of Briarcliff Manor, perhaps it was better this way. I felt closer to the building because I could be there the day she died. She could go the way she lived, impressing those of us who were there on that last day and making headlines.

—Michael Molinelli
Architect, AIA, and volunteer member of the Briarcliff Manor Fire Department

A VIEW FROM CENTRAL DRIVE. The smoke plume rose hundreds of feet in the air and was seen for miles around. The flames rose higher than the tower extension.

A View from the East Entrance. The fire was first reported around 6:40 a.m. It appeared to start near the main entrance and Great Hall and spread throughout the main wing by the time firefighters arrived on the scene. (Photograph by Jack Bakker.)

The West Front, Where the Tower Joined the Main Lodge. The entire 1902 wing was destroyed in the fire. Damage occurred throughout the other wings. Two wooden columns from the ballroom were salvaged later and marked for sale in a New York City antique shop in 2003, offered for together for the sum of $3,700. Some wooden stair railings and door hardware were also salvaged. (Photograph by Jack Bakker.)

A View from the North Wing and Fire Trucks. Over 100 firefighters responded to the blaze, including companies from Bedford, Briarcliff Manor, Croton, Millwood, Ossining, Pleasantville, and Yorktown Heights. (Photograph by Jack Bakker.)

Drawing Water from the Pond. Such a large amount of water was needed to fight the fire that water was drawn from the pond. (Photograph by Jack Bakker.)

THE RUINS OF THE 1902 WING, WEST FRONT. According to investigators who toured the ruins after the blaze, the fire had spread rapidly.

BURNED-OUT GABLE WINDOWS. The fireproof steel-and-concrete construction of the north and west extensions proved their design. These structures did not collapse.

WRECKING THE STONE FACADE. Mazzochi Wrecking of New Jersey arrived in the early afternoon to begin the process of removing the stone facade and fireplace chimneys.

THE 1909 TOWER ABOVE THE RUINS. As of April 2004, no official determination of the cause of fire had been released.

Eight

Walter Law's Briarcliff Manor 2004

The demolition of the remaining sections of Briarcliff Lodge began the afternoon of the fire and continued through the new year until at last the 1980s staircase at the west end of the men's dorm came down and Briarcliff Lodge was no more. All of the buildings on the property have been leveled. Barrington Venture's plan for the site was to build a continuing care retirement community, but as of April 2004, the development was on hold.

Surprisingly, many buildings from Walter Law's Briarcliff Manor survive today. They remain in use as the homes and churches and schools they were built as, while some of the commercial buildings of the Briarcliff Farms have been converted to other use. The contributions of the Law family are still evident in Briarcliff Manor, and their generosity above all else is what longtime residents remember the most. However, when the time came to decide the future of the Briarcliff Lodge property in 2003, the fate of the lodge was still uncertain, and plans for reuse went unrealized.

A similar episode occurred in New York City in 1963, when the classical Pennsylvania Station fell without significant protest. What followed was the beginning of the modern preservation movement. A local landmark movement may or may not occur here because of what happened to Briarcliff Lodge, but we bear the same judgment today as then. Following the demise of the landmark railroad station, the *New York Times* wrote, "We will probably be judged not by the monuments we build but by those we have destroyed."

The Tower, Briarcliff Lodge, January 15, 2004. The fencing surrounding the property was installed two months before Briarcliff Lodge burned. The No Trespassing sign seen here was posted after the fire.

The Site of Briarcliff Lodge, January 16, 2004. The last remaining section of Briarcliff Lodge was the 1980s stairway addition to the tower. It was knocked down on January 16, 2004. Adjacent to the site of this photograph, near the lodge pond, are the shell of small stone building and the foundation ruins of Walter Law's private greenhouses.

BRIARCLIFF FARMS HOUSING, DALMENY ROAD, MARCH 20, 2004. Six wood-frame cottages originally built for workers of Briarcliff Farms still stand on Dalmeny Road. Another three houses stand on Old Briarcliff Road. Similar houses were also built on South State, Pleasantville, and Poplar Roads.

BRIARCLIFF DAIRY BUILDING, WOODSIDE AVENUE, MARCH 20, 2004. This stone building, formerly part of the dairy operations, is currently owned by Consolidated Edison. A similar stone building, formerly the Briarcliff Manor Light and Power Company, also survives under ownership of Consolidated Edison. The Plasmon Company of America, also on Woodside Avenue, is now the home of Briarcliff Classic and Imported Car Services.

THE RECTORY, CHURCH OF ST. THERESA, PLEASANTVILLE ROAD, MARCH 20, 2004. Part of the original Stillman house survives as the rectory for the Church of St. Theresa. North of the church stands a private house that was once the home of the Briarcliff Table Water Company.

THE LABOR UNION'S OFFICE, PLEASANTVILLE ROAD, MARCH 20, 2004. The office of Local No. 137 International Union of Operating Engineers is built from the original stone walls of a Briarcliff Farms office. The union represents operators of heavy equipment for construction work.

BRIARCLIFF CONGREGATIONAL CHURCH, PLEASANTVILLE ROAD, MARCH 20, 2004. The Briarcliff Congregational Church survives. A new parish house and Sunday school were built across South State Road from the church in 1957, and the grounds retain three of Walter Law's Japanese lanterns, one of which stood at Briarcliff Lodge. The church contains Tiffany stained-glass windows donated by Walter Law in memory of his friend William Sloane and his wife, and others.

THE DYSART HOUSE, PLEASANTVILLE ROAD, MARCH 20, 2004. The Dysart House is a private residence today and has recently been restored by its current owners. Walter Law's own Manor House still stands as well. Located on Scarborough Road, it has been a private residence since 1993. His children's homes still stand on the opposite side of Scarborough Road, and farther west on the same road is the All Saints' Episcopal Church.

DOW HALL, ELM ROAD, APRIL 9, 2004. Mrs. Dow's School became Briarcliff Junior College, having been granted its provisional charter in 1935. Pace University acquired the property in 1977, and it is now the school's Briarcliff campus.

BRIARCLIFF MANOR PUBLIC LIBRARY, PLEASANTVILLE ROAD, MARCH 13, 2004. It is possible that a new library may be built, thus leaving the fate of another Walter Law landmark to be decided. When the railroad station was converted to the library, village residents praised the purchase, saving the village the cost of constructing a "flimsy and modern" building.